NEW MERM

General editors:
William C. Carroll, Boston University
Brian Gibbons, University of Münster
Tiffany Stern, University College, University of Oxford

General editor for the Bernard Shaw titles:
L. W. Conolly, Trent University

NEW MERMAIDS

NEW MERMAIDS

BERNARD SHAW

ARMS AND THE MAN

A Pleasant Play

Definitive Text

Edited by J. P. Wearing

Professor Emeritus of English, University of Arizona

Methuen Drama • London

New Mermaids

1 3 5 7 9 10 8 6 4 2

First published 2008

Methuen Drama
A & C Black Publishers Limited
38 Soho Square
London W1D 3HB
www.acblack.com

ISBN 978–0–7136–7998–4

Typeset by RefineCatch Limited, Bungay, Suffolk

CONTENTS

ACKNOWLEDGEMENTS

I am grateful to the Society of Authors, on behalf of the Bernard Shaw Estate, for permission to use the text of *Arms and the Man* and additional Shaw materials quoted in this edition. For permission to use materials in their possession, I am grateful to: the British Library; the Division of Rare and Manuscript Collections, Cornell University Library; the London School of Economics Archives; and the Harry Ransom Humanities Research Center, the University of Texas at Austin. I have received generous assistance from Molly Schwartzburg and Rick Watson (Harry Ransom Humanities Research Center, the University of Texas at Austin), Katherine Reagan (Cornell University Library), Jennie Rathbun (Houghton Library, Harvard University), Susan Donnelly (London School of Economics Archives), Norma Jenckes, Thomas Postlewait, and the staff of the Theatre Museum, London. In addition to the staff of the above-mentioned libraries, I have also received every courtesy from the staff of Bay County Public Library, Panama City, Florida, and Florida State University Library; I am most grateful to them all. Susan Gibbons has been a most collegial and assiduous copy editor and proof reader. Not least, Leonard Conolly has proven an exemplary general editor by providing every advice and encouragement during my work on this edition.

J.P. Wearing

BERNARD SHAW: A CHRONOLOGY

For a comprehensive and detailed chronology of Shaw's life, see A.M. Gibbs, *A Bernard Shaw Chronology* (Basingstoke, 2001). Dates of British and foreign productions of Shaw's plays are given in Raymond Mander and Joe Mitchenson, *Theatrical Companion to Shaw* (New York, 1955), and definitive bibliographical information on Shaw can be found in Dan H. Laurence, *Bernard Shaw: A Bibliography*, 2 vols. (Oxford, 1983).

1856   Born in Dublin, 26 July, to George Carr Shaw and Lucinda Elizabeth Shaw.

1871   Leaves school and takes an office job with a Dublin property agency.

1876   Moves from Dublin to London.

1879   Completes his first novel, *Immaturity* (first published 1930).

1880   Completes his second novel, *The Irrational Knot* (first published in serial form in *Our Corner*, 1885–7, and in book form 1905).

1881   Completes his third novel, *Love Among the Artists* (first published in serial form in *Our Corner*, 1887–8, and in book form 1900).

1883   Completes his fourth and fifth (his last completed) novels, *Cashel Byron's Profession* (first published in serial form in *To-Day*, 1885–6, and in book form 1886) and *An Unsocial Socialist* (first published in serial form in *To-Day*, 1884, and in book form 1887).

1884   Joins the Fabian Society.

1885   Publishes first music and drama criticism in the *Dramatic Review*. Shaw's criticism (including art and literary criticism) also appeared in periodicals such as the *Pall Mall Gazette*, *The World*, and *The Star* before he began a three-year stint as drama critic for the *Saturday Review* (1895–8).

1891   Publishes *The Quintessence of Ibsenism*.

1892   His first play, *Widowers' Houses* (begun 1884) performed by the Independent Theatre Society, London.

1893   Completes *The Philanderer* and *Mrs Warren's Profession*.

1894   *Arms and the Man* performed at the Avenue Theatre, London, and the Herald Square Theatre, New York; completes *Candida*.

1896   Meets Charlotte Payne-Townshend, his future wife. Completes *You Never Can Tell* and *The Devil's Disciple*.

1897   *Candida* performed by the Independent Theatre Company, Aberdeen. *The Man of Destiny* performed at the Grand Theatre, Croydon. American actor Richard Mansfield produces *The Devil's Disciple* in Albany and New York.

1898   Marries Charlotte Payne-Townshend. Publishes (in two volumes) *Plays Pleasant and Unpleasant*, containing four 'pleasant' plays (*Arms and the Man, Candida, The Man of Destiny, You Never Can Tell*) and three 'unpleasant' plays (*Widowers' Houses, The Philanderer, Mrs Warren's Profession*). Completes *Caesar and Cleopatra. Mrs Warren's Profession* is banned by the Lord Chamberlain from public performance in England. Publishes *The Perfect Wagnerite* (on the *Ring* cycle).

1899   *You Never Can Tell* performed by the Stage Society. Writes *Captain Brassbound's Conversion.*

1901   Publishes *Three Plays for Puritans* (*The Devil's Disciple, Caesar and Cleopatra, Captain Brassbound's Conversion*). Writes *The Admirable Bashville.*

1902   *Mrs Warren's Profession* performed (a private production) by the Stage Society.

1903   Publishes *Man and Superman* (begun in 1901).

1904   Begins his partnership with Harley Granville Barker and J.E. Vedrenne at the Royal Court Theatre (until 1907). Eleven Shaw plays are produced there, including *Major Barbara* (1905).

1905   *Mrs Warren's Profession* performed (then banned) in New Haven and New York. *The Philanderer* performed by the New Stage Club, London.

1906   *Caesar and Cleopatra* performed (in German) in Berlin. Publishes *Dramatic Opinions and Essays*, and writes *The Doctor's Dilemma.*

1908   Writes *Getting Married.*

1909   *The Shewing-up of Blanco Posnet* banned in England, but performed in Dublin. *Press Cuttings* banned in England. Completes *Misalliance.*

1911   *Fanny's First Play* performed at the Little Theatre, London. Runs for 622 performances (a record for a Shaw première).

1912   Completes *Pygmalion.*

1913   *Pygmalion* performed (in German) in Vienna.

1914   *Mrs Warren's Profession* performed by the Dublin Repertory Theatre. *Pygmalion* performed at His Majesty's Theatre, London. Outbreak of World War One. Publishes *Common Sense about the War.*

1917   Visits front line sites in France. Completes *Heartbreak House.*
1918   End of World War One.
1920   *Heartbreak House* performed by the Theatre Guild, New York. Completes *Back to Methuselah.*
1922   *Back to Methuselah* performed by the Theatre Guild, New York.
1923   Completes *Saint Joan.* It is performed in New York by the Theatre Guild.
1924   First British production of *Saint Joan,* New Theatre, London. The Lord Chamberlain's ban on *Mrs Warren's Profession* is removed.
1925   First public performances in England of *Mrs Warren's Profession* (in Birmingham and London).
1926   Awarded the 1925 Nobel Prize for Literature.
1928   Publishes *The Intelligent Woman's Guide to Socialism and Capitalism.*
1929   *The Apple Cart* performed (in Polish) in Warsaw, followed by the British première at the Malvern Festival, where other British premières (*Too True to be Good, The Simpleton of the Unexpected Isles, Buoyant Billions*) and world premières (*Geneva* and *In Good King Charles's Golden Days*) of Shaw's plays were produced between 1932 and 1949.
1930   Begins publication of *The Works of Bernard Shaw,* completed (in 33 volumes) in 1938.
1931   Visits Russia; meets Gorky and Stalin.
1933   Writes *On the Rocks.*
1936   *The Millionairess* performed (in German) in Vienna.
1938   *Pygmalion* is filmed, starring Leslie Howard and Wendy Hiller.
1939   Outbreak of World War Two. Wins an Oscar for the screenplay of *Pygmalion.*
1940   *Major Barbara* is filmed, starring Rex Harrison and Wendy Hiller.
1943   Charlotte Shaw dies.
1944   Publishes *Everybody's Political What's What?*
1945   *Caesar and Cleopatra* is filmed, starring Claude Rains and Vivien Leigh. End of World War Two.
1950   Dies, 2 November, aged 94, from complications after a fall while pruning a shrub in his garden. Cremated at Golders Green Crematorium on 6 November, his ashes (mixed with his wife's) scattered at his country home in Ayot St Lawrence, Hertfordshire (now a National Trust property), on 23 November.

ABBREVIATIONS

References to *Arms and the Man* are to the line-numbers of the present edition. The following abbreviations are used throughout this edition.

BL	British Library
CB	Cornell University: the Bernard F. Burgunder Shaw Collection: MS 4617 (bound ms2): first-production prompt copy of the play
CB/R	1894 rehearsal notes and corrections made in CB (above); not in Shaw's hand
CL	Dan H. Laurence, ed. *Bernard Shaw: Collected Letters*, 4 vols., 1965–88
CPB	Bernard F. Dukore, ed. *Bernard Shaw's Arms and the Man: A Composite Production Book*, Carbondale, IL, c.1982
Diaries	Stanley Weintraub, ed. *Bernard Shaw: The Diaries, 1885–1897 with Early Autobiographical Notebooks and Diaries, and an Abortive 1917 Diary*, University Park, PA, 1986
DE	The definitive edition of *Arms and the Man*, published in *The Bodley Head Bernard Shaw: Volume I*, 1970
GR	First English edition of *Arms and the Man* published by Grant Richards, 1898
Halstan	Shaw's postcards to Margaret Halstan critiquing her performance as Raina (Criterion Theatre, London, 18 May 1911); used as cover and inside cover illustrations to Ann L. Ferguson, *'The Instinct of an Artist': Shaw and the Theatre: An Exhibition from the Bernard F. Burgunder Collection of George Bernard Shaw*, Ithaca, NY, 1997 [item 7A in the exhibition]

HL	A typescript of *Arms and the Man* in the Houghton Library, Harvard University (MS Eng 1046.1)
Holroyd	Michael Holroyd, *Bernard Shaw*, 4 vols., New York, 1988–92
HRC	Harry Ransom Humanities Research Center, the University of Texas at Austin
LC	Typescript copy of *Arms and the Man*, submitted in 1894 to the Lord Chamberlain's Office for licensing (BL Add Ms 53546 'O')
LSE	London School of Economics Archives
MS	Original manuscript of *Arms and the Man* written in three notebooks: in the British Library, Add Ms 50601A, 50601B, and 50601C (also published as *Arms and the Man: A Facsimile of the Holograph Manuscript*, Introduction by Norma Jenckes, New York and London, 1981
Theatrics	Dan. H. Laurence, ed., *Theatrics*, Toronto, 1995
US	First North American edition of *Arms and the Man* published Chicago and New York, Herbert S. Stone, 1898

Other Abbreviations

om.	omits, omitted
s.d.	stage direction(s)

INTRODUCTION

The Author

George Bernard Shaw was born on 26 July 1856 in Dublin into a family proud of its connections with the Protestant landed gentry, but enjoying only modest financial circumstances that nevertheless did not preclude employing servants. Shaw's parents, George and Lucinda, were already drifting apart; his father was feckless and his mother interested more in music than her family. Shaw's schooling, which he loathed, was erratic; more significant for his subsequent career was his exposure to music (at home), art (in Dublin's National Gallery), and particularly the theatre. In addition to operas, the local theatres provided a wide array of typical nineteenth-century dramatic fare – Shakespeare, melodramas, French adaptations, dramas and comedies.[1] Shaw read voraciously, discovering the works of John Bunyan, Charles Dickens, Shelley, and Byron. All these sources provided a formative cornerstone that Shaw drew on in his own early works. One other influence was the experience Shaw gained while he worked in an estate office; there he was exposed to some of the grimmer economic and social realities of life.

In 1873 Shaw's mother moved to London, following her musical guru, Vandeleur Lee, and taking her two daughters with her. Shaw followed them in 1876, although he had no visible prospects. His mother provided some support, while Shaw supplemented small contributions from his father by ghost-writing musical criticism for Lee. Shaw soon launched out into other fields, in particular writing novels, and politics – the latter more successfully than the former. His first semi-autobiographical novel, with the inadvertently appropriate title *Immaturity* (1879), was rejected by publishers, as were the four that followed. Some, such as *The Irrational Knot* (1880) and *Cashel Byron's Profession* (1882), were serialised in sympathetic socialist magazines. 1882 was the year in which a lecture by the American economist Henry George awoke Shaw to the importance of economics, which in turn led him to read Karl Marx and to embrace socialism. Shaw rejected his brief flirtation with the Social Democratic Federation in favour of membership in the newly formed Fabian Society (1884) in which he became a prominent and hardworking leading figure. The society wanted to transform England by

---

1 See *Theatrics*, pp. xii–xv. The most recent biographies are A.M. Gibbs, *Bernard Shaw: A Life*, 2005, and Michael Holroyd, *Bernard Shaw*, 4 vols., 1988–92.

gradually permeating social and political institutions, persuading through rational debate and research rather than by revolutionary over-throw. The society introduced Shaw to such life-long friends as Beatrice and Sidney Webb and a whole host of influential people.

Around the same time, while studying opera scores and Marx side-by-side in the Reading Room of the British Museum, Shaw met William Archer, eventually a close friend. The association also turned Shaw into a journalist and critic: he reviewed books for the *Pall Mall Gazette* (1885–8), art and later music for the *World* (1886–94), music for the *Star* (1888–90), and drama for the *Saturday Review* (1895–8). Archer was also responsible for suggesting that they collaborate on adapting a play by the French dramatist Emile Augier, but the project (entitled *Rhinegold*) fell apart because Shaw used up all the plot that Archer provided before completing the play.

However, a few years later and in the midst of a growing interest in new drama encouraged by Ibsen's plays, Shaw found the opportunity to combine his political and social interests by reviving and revising his incomplete play for the recently formed Independent Theatre Society. Now entitled *Widowers' Houses*, Shaw's exposure of slum landlordism attracted mixed responses at the two performances the play received on 9 and 13 December 1892. Although Shaw declared the play produced a sensation and that he was now infamous, there is little contemporary evidence to substantiate his claims.[2] Undeterred, he found his stride, and quickly wrote three more plays, *The Philanderer*, *Mrs Warren's Profession*, and *Arms and the Man*, although only the last was staged immediately. In the following decade theatrical success largely eluded Shaw; nevertheless, he produced several plays on a variety of topics that challenged entrenched contem-porary attitudes and that would eventually find a place in the repertoire. These were *Candida* (first performed 1897), *The Devil's Disciple* (1897), *You Never Can Tell* (1899), and *Captain Brassbound's Conversion* (1900). He also sought audiences by publishing his plays in versions with consider-ably expanded stage directions designed to appeal to readers, and with prefaces in which he expounded his views. *Plays: Pleasant and Unpleasant*, the first in a frequent succession of volumes, was published in 1898, the same year that he married Charlotte Payne-Townshend, a companionable marriage that lasted until her death in 1943.

What really brought Shaw the dramatist to the forefront were the seasons of plays presented at the Royal Court Theatre by J.E. Vedrenne and Harley Granville-Barker, seasons that Shaw underwrote. In addition

2 Holroyd, I, p. 281.

to revivals of earlier plays, Vedrenne and Barker presented *John Bull's Other Island* (1904), *Man and Superman* (1905), *Major Barbara* (1905), and *The Doctor's Dilemma* (1906), adding *Caesar and Cleopatra* in 1907 when they moved briefly to the Savoy Theatre. Then, in the pre-World War I years, Shaw consolidated his position as London's leading dramatist with plays such as *Misalliance* (1910), the very long-running *Fanny's First Play* (1911), *Androcles and the Lion* (1913), and *Pygmalion* (1914), destined to achieve further fame as the musical, *My Fair Lady*.

Shaw's popularity (and his playwriting) waned with the advent of war and his pronouncements in *Common Sense About the War* (1914), whose rationality clashed with the prevailing jingoist mood of the country. He gave his artistic judgement on those responsible for the war in *Heartbreak House* (performed in New York in 1920 and London in 1921), which he described as *A Fantasia in the Russian Manner on English Themes*. A postwar public received it unenthusiastically: the strong cast was rewarded by only 63 performances.[3] The sprawling five-part structure of Shaw's next play, *Back to Methuselah*, even with its more optimistic theme, militated against a popular success; the cycle was played just four times in the 1924 London production. Yet within a month, Shaw's fortunes were reversed when *Saint Joan* achieved 244 performances at the New Theatre (Sybil Thorndike's Joan establishing the benchmark for every subsequent actress); the play is generally regarded as one of Shaw's highest accomplishments.[4] Appropriately, a Nobel Prize followed in 1925, an honour Shaw dismissed, although he accepted the prize so that the prize money might be used for an Anglo-Swedish Literary Foundation.[5]

Although Shaw continued to write plays of some merit (such as *The Apple Cart* [1929] and *The Millionairess* [1936]), the latter third of his career found him much less of a theatrical force. However, his other interests were unabated and the public was usually ready to listen to his encyclopaedic views. Some of these found their way into books such as *The Intelligent Woman's Guide to Socialism and Capitalism* (1928) and *Everybody's Political What's What?* (1944). He travelled extensively, including a controversial trip to Russia in 1931 that revealed his admiration for Stalin (he held similar controversial positions, at least for a time, about Mussolini and Hitler). Nevertheless, he was regarded as something of an oracle right up to his death in 1950.

3   *The Times* (19 October 1921) thought it should be called *Scatterbrain House* and averred: 'As usual with Mr. Shaw, the play is about an hour too long'.

4   *Saint Joan* had also been successful at its première at the Garrick, New York (28 December 1923) with 219 performances.

5   Holroyd, III, pp. 92–4.

Composition

Since honesty in romantic relationships is a major theme in *Arms and the Man*, it is ironic that Shaw's own philandering entanglements were possibly an impetus for the play. In 1893 Shaw was involved with Jenny Patterson, Bertha Newcombe, and Florence Farr. Patterson had provided a twenty-nine year old Shaw with his sexual initiation; eight years later the demanding Patterson no longer fascinated him. Shaw had no ardent interest in Newcombe, yet did not discourage her pursuit of him.[6] More desirable was Farr, in whom Shaw 'appeared to have met a New Woman after his own prescription';[7] the two had been lovers for three years. Scarcely any speculation is entailed in inferring some of the situations and conversations in *Arms and the Man* derive from Shaw's own experience. Moreover, some of Shaw's friends 'served me as models. . . . Bluntschli v. Saranoff–Sidney Webb v. Cunningham Graham in the Socialist movement. Saranoff's "I never withdraw" is historical. It occurred in the House of Commons when Cunningham Graham said "Damn". . . . Raina–Mrs [Annie] Besant'.[8]

Shaw's diary records that on 26 November 1893, after avoiding a meeting with the persistent Jenny Patterson, he began 'a new play – a romantic one – for FE'.[9] Apart from his amorous interest in Florence Farr, Shaw had an additional reason to compose something for her: she had received financial backing from Annie Horniman in order to advance her theatrical career, and Florence had decided to present a season of plays at the Avenue Theatre.[10]

Shaw's disordered manuscript reveals his initial ideas for *Alps and Balkans* (the original title of *Arms and the Man*) were confined to unformed generalities about setting and characters, as Shaw's self-interview in *To-day* (28 April 1894) recounted: 'In the original MS. the names of the places were blank, and the characters were called simply The Father, The Daughter, The

6 See Holroyd, I, pp. 427–9.

7 Holroyd, I, p. 246.

8 *CL*, II, p. 34. Shaw's letter (5 January 1920) to H.C. Duffin provides similar information (BL Add Ms 50518, f. 195v). William Archer saw autobiographical parallels and identified Shaw with Bluntschli (*Study and Stage: A Year-book of Criticism*, 1899, p. 4). See also Louis Crompton's discussion of Cunninghame Graham and Sidney Webb in *Shaw the Dramatist: A Study of the Intellectual Background of the Major Plays*, 1971, pp. 21–3.

9 *Diaries*, p. 989. 'FE' indicates Farr's married name, Florence Emery. See also Shaw's account of the composition and reception of *Arms and the Man* in Samuel A. Weiss, ed., *Bernard Shaw's Letters to Siegfried Trebitsch*, 1986, pp. 76–7.

10 Annie Horniman also financed the Abbey Theatre, Dublin, in 1904, and in 1907 established the first repertory theatre in England at Manchester. Shaw did not learn of her involvement in the Avenue venture until 1904 (*CL*, II, p. 452).

Stranger, The Heroic Lover, and so on'.[11] Moreover, Shaw's methods were haphazard: on 28 November, when at a loose end, he 'went into the park and sat there working at the new play' for an hour or so. The next evening he 'worked at the new play between the acts' of a performance of Sheridan's *The School of Scandal*.[12] He completed Act I in December, only to be distracted by a Christmas holiday with Sidney and Beatrice Webb, during which he drafted a Fabian Society manifesto. Twice Farr wrote anxiously to Shaw 'reproaching me vigorously for not having worked at the play for her. So I set to and wrote 12 pages of it'.[13] More fitful attempts followed, as did reading extracts to various friends.[14] February and March found Shaw either tinkering with the play 'on my out to Ravenscourt Park' to see Farr, or working 'vigorously' for a morning.[15] The process was not effortless, and Shaw suffered occasional indecision: 'Although many of the cancelled words and phrases merely testify to Shaw's sensitivity to redundancy, some manifest more profound dissatisfactions. ... [Notebook] B, folios 20 and 21, which contain the discarded opening to Act III, reveal an almost unthinkable literary phenomenon – Bernard Shaw at a loss for words'.[16]

Shaw was also at a loss for a suitable war to provide a backdrop for the play, although the Balkans of his title had long been an area of contention, particularly between the Russian and Ottoman empires, into which Britain had been drawn, particularly in the Crimean War (1854–6). 'The incident of the machine-gun bound me to a recent war; that was all. My own historical information being rather confused, I asked Mr. Sidney Webb to find out a good war for my purpose. He spent about two minutes in a rapid survey of every war that has ever been waged, and then told me that the Servo-Bulgarian [*sic*] was what I wanted'.[17] Shaw acquired more specific information (including the fact

---

11 Shaw's account is not strictly accurate: he had named some of the characters – Juana (later Raina), Michaeloff (Nicola), and Stanca or Luga (Louka).

12 *Diaries*, p. 990.

13 *Diaries*, p. 1005. Earlier (2 January 1894) he 'wrote a scrap of the play, as to which my conscience has been aroused by a letter from FE' (*Diaries*, p. 1003).

14 Shaw read to various friends on 2, 9, 16, 18 December 1893, and 23–4 January 1894 (*Diaries*, pp. 992, 994, 996–7). He worked on the play on 11 and 15 January (*Diaries*, pp. 1005–06, 1008).

15 *Diaries*, pp. 1011, 1018.

16 Norma Jenckes, 'Introduction', *Arms and the Man: A Facsimile of the Holograph Manuscript*, 1981, pp. xvii, xix.

17 *To-day*, 28 April 1894. Ronald Bryden argues convincingly that Shaw had already fixed on the Balkan setting and was partly inspired by newspaper reports of the death of Prince Alexander 'on November 18 [1893], the eighth anniversary of the battle of Slivnitza in which he had led his nation to victory over the Serbs' (*Shaw and His Contemporaries*, 2002, p. 9).

that Serbia had not won the war, as he had thought) on 17 March 1894 when he read the play to fellow Socialist Sergius Stepniak and a 'Russian who commanded the Bulgarian fleet during the war'.[18] As a result, 'I have had to shift the scene from Servia [*sic*] to Bulgaria, and to make the most absurd alterations in detail for the sake of local color, which, however, is amusing & will intensify the extravagance of the play & give it realism at the same time'.[19] Shaw went 'to the [British] Museum where I sat until near 19 [7 p.m.] reading up the account of the Servo-Bulgarian War in the *Annual Register*, and studying maps of the Balkan Peninsula'.[20] On 27 March Shaw tried out a virtually complete version of *Arms and the Man* on Bertha Newcombe: 'After dinner [lunch] we went out and sat on a bank all the afternoon, I reading the play, which she did not like at all'.[21] Conceivably, Bertha perceived and disliked aspects of herself, Shaw, and their relationship in what she heard.

Two days later theatrical fate intervened. Farr's opening production at the Avenue on 29 March 1894 (John Todhunter's *A Comedy of Sighs*) failed; the next day Shaw found Farr and her acting manager, C.T.H. Helmsley, considering his *Widowers' Houses* as a replacement. Shaw 'dissuaded them from that and after some discussion took my new play out on to the Embankment Gardens and there and then put the last touches to it before leaving it to be typewritten'.[22] *Arms and the Man* went into production and, inexperienced in such matters, Shaw consulted a theatre friend (Charles Charrington) on the terms he should agree to: 'I do not want to use my influence with F.F. to get more than my due; and on the other [hand] I do not want to blackleg dramatic authordom by taking too little & running down prices'.[23] Recruiting a cast required coaxing some actors into

18 *Diaries*, p. 1019. Stepniak was a Soviet socialist friend; the Russian was Admiral Esper Aleksandrovich Serebryekov. Shaw gave an expansive account of these events in the *Pall Mall Budget*, 19 April 1894.

19 *Theatrics*, p. 12.

20 *Diaries*, p. 1020 (19 March). Shaw recorded some one hundred words from *The Annual Register: A Review of Public Events at Home and Abroad for the Year 1885*, 1886, pp. 267–78 in his Notebook A. Maurice Valency notes 'it is difficult to see . . . why further research was necessary. *Arms and the Man* did not need careful documentation. Its detail and its coloring were purely theatrical' (*The Cart and the Trumpet: The Plays of George Bernard Shaw*, 1973, p. 106).

21 *Diaries*, p. 1022.

22 *Diaries*, p. 1023. *A Comedy of Sighs* was withdrawn on 14 April after 16 performances. W.B. Yeats' accompanying one-act, *The Land of Heart's Desire*, was suspended until *Arms and the Man* was produced, and was withdrawn on 12 May after 35 performances altogether.

23 *Theatrics*, p. 11. Shaw drew up an agreement proposing royalties on a sliding scale of 5, 7$\frac{1}{2}$, and 10% of gross receipts (HRC, Shaw/Box 3.6), but it was not effected, and he received a 5% royalty.

accepting specific roles before rehearsals began on 11 April, just ten days before opening night.[24] Even so, Shaw continued to amend the play; when the typescript (dated 31 March 1894) was submitted to the Lord Chamberlain for licensing, it still bore the title *Alps and Balkans*, as did revised typescripts prepared in early April for rehearsals. By 13 April Shaw had changed the title to *Arms and the Man* since he used that title in the 'interview' he drafted for *The Star* (14 April 1894).[25] This first-production text differs considerably from later versions, as one of countless examples demonstrates. The manuscript stage direction for Sergius' first entrance reads: '*Enter Nicola L, followed by Sergius*'. When Shaw finalized the definitive text in 1930, Sergius' entrance had burgeoned into thirty lines of novelistic description (II, 242–71) that allow Shaw to introduce multifarious ideas and suggestions about Sergius' character. It is a moot point whether these were Shaw's original thoughts or whether they were generated by rehearsals or other influences.

Influences and Sources

Allusions and parallels in *Arms and the Man* abound; indeed, in his Preface to *Three Plays for Puritans* (1901), Shaw acknowledged that *Arms and the Man* employed 'the forgotten [stage tricks] of the sixties' (he claimed, inaccurately, that the play's 'real novelty, which nobody off the stage noticed, was that Major Petkoff's library had only one door').[26] In fact, Shaw's early plays, 'so far from being new, are a tissue of reminiscences of earlier work' by dramatists such as H.A. Jones, Arthur Pinero, Bulwer Lytton, T.W. Robertson, H.J. Byron, and Dion Boucicault; and Martin Meisel has demonstrated meticulously how Shaw and his drama were steeped in the nineteenth-century theatrical tradition.[27] Ironically,

24 See letter to Alma Murray 30 March 1894, *CL*, I, p. 422. The *Diaries* (pp. 1024–5) record seven rehearsals between 11 and 20 April, but there may have been ten (*Shaw on Theatre*, ed. E.J. West, 1958, p. 157). On pre-performance preparations, see also Irving McKee, 'Bernard Shaw's Beginnings on the London Stage', *PMLA*, 74 (1959), 470–71.

25 The Lord Chamberlain issued a licence on 16 April with the new title. Shaw had also considered the following titles: 'Emperor of Switzerland', 'Drums in the Rose Valleys', 'A Choice of Heroes', 'Indomitable!', 'There is But one Step –', 'But One Step', 'A Son of Mars', 'Two Sons of Mars'. Henry Salt, a friend, had suggested 'Battlefields and Boudoirs' (Jenckes, p. xiii, and Henry S. Salt, *Company I Have Kept*, 1930, p. 205). On the variant texts of the play, see 'A Note on the Text', below p. xlviii.

26 *Three Plays for Puritans*, 1949, p. xxv; *CL*, II, p. 686. The same Preface outlines Shaw's concept of the play, 'with its comedic conflict between the knightly Bulgarian and the Mommsenite Swiss captain', p. xxxvii), as a reflection of the differing philosophical perspectives of historians Thomas Carlyle and Theodor Mommsen.

27 Allardyce Nicoll, *A History of English Drama 1660–1900: Volume V: Late Nineteenth-Century Drama 1850–1900*, 1967, p. 194, and Meisel, *Shaw and the Nineteenth-Century Theater*, 1963.

while Shaw ridiculed the French well-made play tradition in his article, 'Sardooledom',[28] he took many cues from its leading exponents, Victorien Sardou and Eugène Scribe. As Stephen S. Stanton has noted: 'The evidence suggests that Shaw availed himself of as many of the tricks and devices of the popular stagecraft of Scribe as would help him to successfully establish on the stage his early plays from *Widowers' Houses* (1892) to *Man and Superman*'. Specifically, '*Arms and the Man* is an ingenious reworking of Scribe's *Bataille de Dames*, the plot of which is first sketched in *A Peculiar Position*'.[29] So, although Shaw's ideas have an iconoclastic twist, they are conveyed in conventional dramatic vehicles.

While Shaw's title evokes Virgil's epic poem the *Aeneid* – it is a translation of Virgil's opening words, 'arma virumque' – Shaw professed that he was espousing the work of the leader of French Romanticism, Victor Hugo, who rejected established rules and restrictions on dramatic composition:

> I have made a desperate attempt to begin a real romantic play for F.F. in the style of Victor Hugo. The first act is nearly finished; and it is quite the funniest attempt at that style of composition ever made. I am told that I have unconsciously reproduced the bedroom scene from [Hugo's] *Marion de L'Orme* [*sic*], which I never read.[30]

Shaw's informant here remains tantalizingly unknown; however, Shaw was possibly offering a retort to his erstwhile dramatic collaborator, William Archer, who had written: 'but what modern dramatist of note, in France or elsewhere, traces his theatrical ancestry to Hugo?' Archer had also observed that 'the foundations of the new drama' derive from Scribe: 'From him, by way of imitation, development, and reaction, the modern drama springs'.[31]

---

28 *Saturday Review*, 1 June 1895.

29 'Shaw's Debt to Scribe', *PMLA*, 76 (1961), 575; and, 'Introduction', '*Camille' and Other Plays*, 1957, p. xxxviii. *A Peculiar Position* (or *A Scrap of Paper*) is a translation of *La Frontière de Savoie* by Scribe and J.F.A. Bayard. See similar points by Eric Bentley, 'The Making of a Dramatist (1892–1903)', in R.J. Kaufmann, ed., *G.B. Shaw: A Collection of Critical Essays*, 1965, pp. 58–9, and Michel Pharand, *Bernard Shaw and the French*, 2000, pp. 57–60.

30 *CL*, I, p. 409. Irving McKee, op. cit., p. 470, compares Shaw's original title, *Alps and Balkans*, with Hugo's *Alpes et Pyrenées*. Shaw had read Hugo's *Les Misérables* in March and April 1893 (Pharand, op. cit., p. 2). On Virgilian parallels, see Calvin T. Higgs, jr., 'Shaw's Use of Vergil's *Aeneid* in *Arms and the Man*', *Shaw Review*, 19 (1976), 2–16. A.M. Gibbs suggests Shaw's friend, Pakenham Thomas Beatty, may have provided a hint for the title (*Shaw: A Life*, p. 89).

31 *About the Theatre: Essays and Studies*, 1886, p. 297. Archer's book includes two chapters, 'The Plays of Victor Hugo', and 'Hugo and Wagner'.

Although *Marion de Lorme* is essentially a courtesan play, some of its incidents are echoed in *Arms and the Man*. Act I is set in Marion's bedroom into which her artless lover, Didier, climbs via a balcony. Like Raina, Marion reads a book while there is an off-stage sword-fight (I.ii), an event replaced by gunfire in *Arms and the Man*. Marion's declaration 'Vous êtes mon Didier, mon maître et mon seigneur' (III.vi) shares the same quality as Sergius' and Raina's avowals: 'My lady and my saint! . . . My lord and my –' (II, 476–8). Hugo's *Hernani*, recast as the libretto for Verdi's 1844 opera *Ernani* (mentioned by Raina, I, 694), provides a source for the harboured fugitive theme, triangular love relationships, and 'the point of honour by which the claims of hospitality outweigh enmity' that are found in *Arms and the Man*.[32] Vincent Wallace's *Maritana* (1845) is another opera that fuses similar thematic ingredients; its English libretto was based on Adolphe Dennery and P.F.P. Dumanoir's *Don César de Bazan*, a melodrama inspired by Hugo's play *Ruy Blas* (1838). Significant is the moment when Don César arrives to rescue his wife: 'A shot rings out, and the figure of a man enters precipitately by a window at a balcony upstage – an entrance Bernard Shaw borrowed for his travesty of romantic heroics'.[33] Meisel, in stressing 'the connection between romantic love and romantic heroism' in *Arms and the Man*, identifies *The Daughter of the Regiment* – an opera (1840) by Donizetti and also an operatic drama (1843) by Edward Fitzball – as the 'quintessential military romance in its fusion of love and heroism', and a source for Shaw's play.[34]

Comparable sources are found in Shakespeare's work, most obviously the balcony (and offstage bedroom) scene in *Romeo and Juliet* (II.ii). There Romeo, an enemy Montague, is a 'fugitive' from his friends; however, in a role inversion, as a romantic young lover he resembles Raina in her excesses and Juliet the more practical Bluntschli. A bedroom variation occurs in *Cymbeline* (II.ii) when, after reading a book, Imogen falls asleep and the villain Iachimo, instead of entering from a balcony, emerges from a trunk.[35] *Coriolanus*, suggested by the rare use of 'acclamations' by both

32 A.M. Gibbs, *The Art and Mind of Shaw: Essays in Criticism*, 1983, pp. 70. Shaw acknowledged the ubiquity of the fugitive theme: 'the incident of a fugitive soldier taking refuge in a lady's bedroom was too common to be patented by me or anyone else' (*Advice to a Young Critic and Other Letters*, ed. E.J. West, 1955, p. 202). In the play, Raina signals the theme blatantly: 'This is the happiest night of my life – if only there are no fugitives' (I, 152–3).

33 Frank Rahill, *The World of Melodrama*, 1967, p. 78. *Don César* is discussed on pp. 75–82.

34 Meisel, op. cit., pp. 186–7. Meisel also discusses the fugitive in a woman's bedroom in Thomas Morton's *The Angel in the Attic* (1843), and Tom Taylor's *Lady Clancarty* (1874), pp. 192–4.

35 Shaw was thoroughly familiar with *Cymbeline* as evidenced by his advice in 1896 to Ellen Terry when she played Imogen at the Lyceum Theatre with Henry Irving (*CL*, I, pp. 646–56, 661–2, 665–6).

Shakespeare and Shaw, presents a divergent heroic fugitive, albeit but briefly: Coriolanus enters the city of Corioli alone 'and is shut in'. While there, 'I sometime lay ... at a poor man's house; he used me kindly' (I.ix.81–2). Both Coriolanus and Sergius fight against considerable odds and observe codes of honour. Another Shakespearean military example is perhaps parodied as Raina describes her pride: 'When I buckled on Sergius's sword he looked so noble: it was treason to think of disillusion or humiliation or failure' (I, 89–90). In *Antony and Cleopatra* (IV.iv) Cleopatra attempts to buckle on Antony's armour, her incompetence inviting comic interpretations.[36]

The military melodramatic romance tradition is encapsulated in *Held by the Enemy*, William Gillette's American civil war drama that Shaw reviewed twice in 1887.[37] In addition to the fugitive soldier motif, *Held by the Enemy* includes windows left unfastened, candles blown out, a cavalry brigade and charge, and a colonel who resigns his commission (though not for the same reasons as Sergius).[38] Another war play well-known to Shaw was T.W. Robertson's *Ours* (1866).[39] Robertson's extensive stage directions, like Shaw's, embody minute realism, and Angus the soldier prefigures Bluntschli:

> '... *a hut, built of boulders and mud, the roof built out, showing the snow and sky outside. The walls bare and rude, pistols, swords, guns, maps, newspapers, etc., suspended on them. ...* ANGUS *discovered, very shabby, high, muddy boots, beard, etc., seated at table, reading by light of candle letters which are lying on an open travelling-desk.*[40]

Ultimately a comedy, *Ours* does not achieve the grim effects of later plays such as R.C. Sheriff's *Journey's End* (1928) or Bertolt Brecht's *Mother Courage and Her Children* (1941); but neither does *Arms and the Man*.

---

36 For parallels between Bluntschli as Falstaff and Sergius as Hotspur, see Robert C. Elliott, 'Shaw's Captain Bluntschli: A Latter-Day Falstaff', *Modern Language Notes*, 67 : 7 (1952), 461–4.

37 *The Drama Observed: Volume I: 1880–1895*, ed. Bernard F. Dukore, 1993, pp. 72–4. Dixie King, 'Bernard Shaw and William Gillette', *English Literature in Transition (1880–1920)*, 27 : 3 (1984), 239–241, discusses some parallels, but is unaware Shaw had reviewed the play. As some first-night reviewers noted, the presence of Alma Murray and Yorke Stephens in both productions reinforced the connection.

38 *Held by the Enemy*, 1898, pp. 29, 53, 102.

39 As a boy Shaw saw *Ours* in Dublin, and also saw a London revival in May 1876 (*Theatrics*, p. xv; Gibbs, *Shaw: A Life*, pp. 77–8).

40 William Tydeman, ed., *Plays by Tom Robertson*, 1982, pp. 114–15. Notably, this scene in Act III has only one entrance (cf. Shaw's remark on p. xix). In Robertson's *War* (1871) a character declares: 'And I tell you that glory is a delusion, a snare, a cruel lie! It means burnt homesteads, ruined villages, abandoned homes, desolation and despair' (Act I).

Although Shaw dismissed comparisons with W.S. Gilbert's work, parallels are readily apparent.[41] *The Pirates of Penzance* (1879) combines military and romantic matters, and age is a determining plot element as it is in *Arms and the Man*.[42] Class discrepancies between Ralph and Josephine propel *H.M.S. Pinafore* (1878); social considerations figure significantly with the Petkoffs, Nicola and Louka, and are a vital ingredient in the play's outcome. *The Yeomen of the Guard* (1888) emphasizes military bravery as epitomized in Elsie's declaration: 'I love all brave men. . . . I love the bravest best' (Act II). Facets of Gilbert's play, *Tom Cobb* (1875), are virtually replicated in *Arms and the Man*. Its heroine (Caroline), of 'poetical demeanour', sends her poet-soldier a photograph, hoping for 'A vast, vast, vast war! Oh for the clash of steel-clad foemen! Oh for the deadly cannonade! And loud above the din of battle, I hear my Arthur's voice, as, like a doughty Paladin of old, he cleaves his path where'er the fight is thickest!' (Act III). Tom Cobb, wearing 'a very low lie-down collar in order to look Byronic', wins Caroline's affection by declaring 'you loved me as a penniless, but poetical major-general; can you still love me as a wealthy, but unromantic apothecary?' (Act III). Archibald Henderson notes that Nicola advising Louka 'to gain a hold over Sergius, marry him ultimately, and so "come to be one of my grandest customers, instead of only being my wife and costing me money" [III, 479–80], is but a paraphrase and inversion of that ludicrous scene in *Engaged*, in which "puir little Maggie Macfarlane" advises her lover, Angus Macalister, to resign Cheviot-Hill for the princely consideration of two pounds'.[43] Finally, confessional truth-telling permeates both *Arms and the Man* and Gilbert's *The Palace of Truth* (1870).

Shaw did acknowledge other influences, although not all those noted above. He called Sergius 'my Bulgarian Don Quixote', took facts from the *Memoirs* (trans. 1892) of General Baron de Marbot, and discovered realistic details of battles in Emile Zola's novel, *Le Débâcle* (trans. 1892).[44] Shaw's resultant play is a magpie's theatrical assemblage.

The Play

In essence, *Arms and the Man* is but a 'well-made play'. Act I provides the romantic premise when the heroine (Raina) encounters a fugitive enemy

---

41 Arthur Sullivan's music for the comic operettas obviously lightens the import and perception of Gilbert's lyrics and libretto.

42 See note to III, 1105. The on-stage portrayal of Major-General Stanley in *Pirates* provoked contemporary associations with Sir Garnet Wolseley (see p. xxxix below).

43 *George Bernard Shaw: His Life and Works*, 1911, p. 313. This scene was also cited by the *Daily News*, 23 April 1894. Gilbert's *Engaged* was first performed in 1877.

44 See 'A Dramatic Realist to His Critics', *New Review*, 9 (July 1894); rpt. in DE, pp. 485–511.

soldier (Bluntschli) and helps him escape using her father's coat as a disguise. Complications ensue in Act II when the heroine's fiancé and her father (Sergius and Petkoff) return from the war: the fiancé has a roving eye for a servant girl (Louka), and he and the father reveal that they encountered Bluntschli during the war. Coincidentally and conveniently, the soldier arrives to return the borrowed coat, heightening expectations of plot complications. In Act III questions about the coat, a photograph, and Raina's age are resolved, a letter bestows an appropriately large fortune on Bluntschli, and impediments to connubial bliss for the two couples are removed.

Arms and the Man is also about the characteristics of relationships and self-knowledge into which notions of warfare, chivalry, romance, idealism, class structure, social prejudices, and economics are woven. From this perspective the two married Petkoffs are stable, but not unreservedly admirable, figures: they are steadfastly grounded in every facet of their lives and their entrenched snobbery: Catherine can declare proudly, 'Our position is almost historical' (III, 1147–8). Nicola, whom Bluntschli declares is 'the ablest man I've met in Bulgaria' (III, 1016–17), is content and secure in his subservient position; he acknowledges his social status, and pragmatically relinquishes his attachment to Louka but not his economic objectives.[45] Louka, though lacking Nicola's worldliness, spurns social distinctions, and practices her seductive wiles to achieve her romantic and economic objectives. Superficially, Bluntschli is the most practical character; a mercenary, he joined the first army that came his way, and he relishes assisting his former enemies in resolving military logistical problems. He possesses a keen insight into warfare, economics, and people. However, his confession of his inveterate 'incurably romantic disposition' connects him with the idealistic romantics, Raina and Sergius. They engage in a radical, apparently enlightened, shift from their fictionalized 'higher love' to imminent marriage with mates of differing social status.

While many of these ideas are commonplace in literature, Shaw renders them more intriguing by employing interlocking literary devices such as paradox, fictive and meta-theatrical allusions, and rhetorical figures. Rather than intensifying a sense of realism, these devices tend to render the play more illusory, more obviously fictional and theatrical.[46]

---

45 See also Bernard F. Dukore, 'The Ablest Man in Bulgaria', *SHAW: The Annual of Shaw Studies*, 22 (2002), 68–82. Archer maintained 'The servants . . . are the subtlest psychologists of the whole band, and are equipped with a perfectly definite and articulate philosophy of life' (*Study and Stage*, p. 13).

46 Margery M. Morgan has observed 'The mechanical toy-shop quality of the entertainment . . . It is a nursery play by virtue of its theme as well as its style' (*The Shavian Playground: An Exploration of the Art of George Bernard Shaw*, 1972, p. 51).

Even though the title *Arms and the Man* was somewhat fortuitous, it reflects Shaw's methodology in the play. As a translation of Virgil's 'arma virumque', the title assumes an allusive, transformational quality; moreover, both works are indebted to earlier sources. Paradoxically, the play is no classical heroic epic poem about mythic characters who have waged war; rather, *Arms and the Man* is predominantly a mixture of romantic and domestic comedy, and although a specific war provides a backdrop, war itself is discussed, not enacted (a technique Shaw employed again in *Saint Joan*). The most realistic details are Bluntschli's costume ('*bespattered with mud and blood and snow, his belt and the strap of his revolver-case keeping together the torn ruins of the blue tunic of a Serbian artillery officer*' I, 205–8), a few gun shots, and the description of Bluntschli's comrade burnt alive: 'Shot in the hip in a woodyard. Couldnt drag himself out. Your fellows' shells set the timber on fire and burnt him, with half a dozen other poor devils in the same predicament' (III, 730–2).

Shaw's paradoxical strategy is further embodied in the stage directions.[47] Act I is historically and geographically specific (November 1885, Bulgaria), yet a fairy-tale quality obtains: the romantic bedroom balcony looks out on the mountain peak that, '*wonderfully white and beautiful in the starlit snow, seems quite close at hand, though it is really miles away*' (I, 3–5). That picture-postcard effect simultaneously exposes the illusory quality of theatrical scenery. The bedroom is filled with contradictions: rich Bulgarian/cheap Viennese, a shrine and Christ image/a Turkish ottoman, oriental and gorgeous fabrics/occidental and paltry wallpaper, common pine table/expensive toilet mirror. Prominent is '*a miniature easel with a large photograph of an extremely handsome officer, whose lofty bearing and magnetic glance can be felt even from the portrait*' (I, 24–6). Like the background scenery, this photograph is not the thing itself, only a representation that ostensibly captures Sergius' character; however, one purpose of the play (itself a fiction) is to peel away what the photograph embodies, exposing it as a sham. 'News' (only ever a report of something) reveals that Sergius has become the 'idol of the regiment' (I, 61), a concept that connects him with the Christ icon and worship, inherently a theatrical activity. Convolutedly, Raina declares this news 'proves that our ideas were real after all' (I, 81–2); in fact, Raina and Sergius have founded their ideas, their very existence, on reading Byron and Pushkin, and on operas staged in Bucharest. Even as late as Act III, 29–30 '*Raina, reclining on the divan, is gazing in a daydream out at the Balkan landscape, with a*

---

47 This discussion refers to the definitive text. However, Shaw's first thoughts as represented in his manuscript or early prompt scripts were not necessarily fully formed.

neglected novel in her lap'. Clearly, both have formulated their lives on the fictional, not reality, a characteristic reflected in Raina's linguistic choices: 'Yes: I was only a prosaic little coward. Oh, to think that it was all true! that Sergius is just as splendid and noble as he looks! that the world is really a glorious world for women who can see its glory and men who can act its romance! What happiness! what unspeakable fulfilment!' (I, 111–15). Raina moves from the prosaic to the romantic, and then into a metatheatrical world in which Sergius can 'act', but his (unseen) glorious world, ironically, comprises death and destruction.

The preface to Raina's entanglement with the war is similarly cloaked in idolatry and fiction:

> RAINA [*looking up at the picture*]
> Oh, I shall never be unworthy of you any more, my soul's hero: never, never, never. [*She replaces it reverently. Then she selects a novel from the little pile of books. She turns over the leaves dreamily; finds her page; turns the book inside out at it; and, with a happy sigh, gets into bed and prepares to read herself to sleep. But before abandoning herself to fiction, she raises her eyes once more, thinking of the blessed reality, and murmurs*] My hero! my hero!
>
> (I, 170–7)

The subsequent scene is a re-enactment of a well-worn theatrical and operatic theme (harbouring a fugitive soldier) that converts the remainder of Act I into unequivocal meta-theatricality. While the fugitive Bluntschli is described in realistic terms, the description is but a theatrical borrowing (see above, p. xxii). Bluntschli's language is realistic: 'A lot of your cavalry will burst into this pretty room of yours and slaughter me here like a pig; for I'll fight like a demon: they shant get *me* into the street to amuse themselves with'(I, 239–42). However, the scene in which he hides behind a curtain to avoid detection and inadvertently leaves his gun on the bed is a rudimentary theatrical routine. Sound though some of Bluntschli's observations on warfare might be, his famous defence of carrying chocolate instead of bullets is fatuous and exposes 'the traditional comedic framework Shaw adopts. The chocolate creams in Bluntschli's cartridge case are what give the show away – the real Shavian soldier would have carried an *extra* supply of bullets'.[48] However, neither Bluntschli nor his creator is against war itself, as G.K. Chesterton observed shrewdly:

48 Alfred Turco, jr., *Shaw's Moral Vision: The Self and Salvation*, 1976, p. 88. The possibility that this idea may have been borrowed from a Pinero farce reinforces the point (see note to I, 421–3).

Shaw has many of the actual opinions of Tolstoy. Like Tolstoy he tells men, with coarse innocence, that romantic war is only butchery and that romantic love is only lust. But Tolstoy objects to these things because they are real; he really wishes to abolish them. Shaw only objects to them in so far as they are ideal; that is in so far as they are idealised. Shaw objects not so much to war as to the attractiveness of war. He does not so much dislike love, as the love of love. Before the temple of Mars Tolstoy stands and thunders 'There shall be no wars'; Bernard Shaw merely murmurs, 'Wars if you must; but for God's sake, not war songs'.[49]

When the focus in Act I reverts to Sergius and his heroic charge, Bluntschli fictionalizes him: 'He did it like an operatic tenor. A regular handsome fellow, with flashing eyes and lovely moustache, shouting his war-cry and charging like Don Quixote at the windmills' (I, 515–17). (The Quixote allusion, employed three times, is reinforced by Raina using Sergius's photograph as a means of identifying him to Bluntschli.) However, Bluntschli himself is swiftly recast when Raina moulds him into the 'chocolate cream soldier',[50] recalls his (theatrical) balcony-climbing, and correlates Bluntschli's escapade with the opera *Ernani*: 'I thought you might have remembered the great scene where Ernani, flying from his foes just as you are tonight, takes refuge in the castle of his bitterest enemy, an old Castilian noble. The noble refuses to give him up. His guest is sacred to him' (I, 703–6). This speech deftly introduces the theme of honour and hospitality, itself a much repeated literary theme. Furthermore, the whole of Bluntschli's Act I encounter is presented fictively when Petkoff and Sergius narrate it in Act II, describing it as 'that queer story' and 'quite a romance' (II, 394, 398).

The Act II stage directions resemble those for Act I. The precise date, 6 March 1886, invests the scene with historical realism, although the information depends on audiences reading their programmes. The Petkoffs'

---

49 G.K. Chesterton, *George Bernard Shaw*, 1910; rpt. 1956, pp. 88–9. G. Wilson Knight, *The Golden Labyrinth*, 1962, p. 347, points out 'Shaw likes soldiers', in such plays as *Arms and the Man*, *Too True to be Good*, *The Devil's Disciple*, *Androcles and the Lion*, and *Caesar and Cleopatra*. Gordon N. Bergquist analyzes Shaw's views on war in *The Pen and the Sword: War and Peace in the Prose and Plays of Bernard Shaw*, 1977. Shaw's articles on World War I are collected in *What I Really Wrote About the War*, 1932, described as 'by far the most confused writing he ever did' (J. Percy Smith, *The Unrepentant Pilgrim: A Study of the Development of Bernard Shaw*, 1965, p. 155).

50 'Chocolate! Do you stuff your pockets with *sweets* – like a schoolboy – even in the field?' (I, 425–6). When Bluntschli is reintroduced in Act II, he is associated with chocolate (706, 732, 878), as well as the borrowed coat (698–9, 766), and the balcony scene itself (714).

social ambiguity is captured in the '*washing spread out to dry*' on the fruit bushes (II, 10), while the opening duologue between Louka and Nicola incorporates lower social class considerations.

Meta-theatrical are the discernible parallels with the beginning of Ibsen's *Ghosts* (1881). The set for *Ghosts* is a 'garden room' with a backdrop of 'a gloomy fjord landscape'; *Arms and the Man* is set in a garden, and in the distance '*the Balkan mountains rise and shut in the landscape*' (II, 5). Louka's headstrong personality, reinforced by her socially audacious act of smoking a cigarette, is comparable to Regine's, and both women entertain notions of upward social mobility. Nicola, who sees his 'soul of a servant' as 'the secret of success in service', plans on opening 'a shop in Sofia' (II, 81–3, 40). The more wayward Engstrand has a similar objective 'of starting a sort of tavern – for seamen –'. Each pair enjoys an ambiguous relationship that changes as a result of plot manipulations: Engstrand and Regine begin as ostensibly father and daughter, Nicola and Louka as engaged to be married. Both shifts are effected by family secrets, and Osvald's seduction of Regine (*Ghosts*, Act I) parallels Sergius' of Louka. As happened with characters in Act I, Nicola and Louka are defined in fictional terms.

Some sense of reality is provided with the interposing of the Petkoffs before the reunion of Raina and Sergius, although Catherine's appearance is paradoxical: she wears a 'half worn-out dressing gown', yet possesses an 'astonishingly handsome and stately' manner (II, 130, 132–3). Catherine and her husband are comfortably bourgeois, solid in social and economic terms, and suffused with snobbery. Even though her husband has just returned from war, 'she stoops over the back of his chair to kiss him', a homely act rather than an effusive display (II, 135–6), and a repetition of Raina doing likewise with Bluntschli (I, 592–3). She dominates her husband, takes inordinate pride in the newly installed electric bell, and shares Raina's ideas on romance and chivalry. Petkoff, though occasionally bumbling, exhibits a practical side with some insight, as when he deflates Catherine by criticizing the washing on the bushes.

These two vignettes increase anticipation by delaying the arrival of the hero, Sergius, a taxing role, Shaw thought:

> Sergius is not a ridiculous personage, sent on the stage to be laughed at, but a superb man, brave, haughty, high-spirited, magnetic and handsome. The difficulty lies, not in finding an actor with these qualifications, but in inducing him to play a part in which all his attractions are reduced to tragic absurdity.[51]

51 Shaw's 'Instructions to Producer', HRC, Shaw/Box 4.1.

Like Bluntschli, Sergius is defined fictively and in extensive novelistic stage directions alluding to Byron and his poem, *Childe Harold*. Sergius is *'the original of the portrait ... romantically handsome ... [with] ... the susceptible imagination of an untamed mountaineer chieftain ... [a] clever imaginative barbarian ... he has acquired the half tragic, half ironic air, the mysterious moodiness, the suggestion of a strange and terrible history that has left nothing but undying remorse'* (II, 242–65). Significantly, Childe Harold, a pilgrim wanderer, is Byron's self-fictionalization, while the poem employs the Spenserian stanza form, thereby evoking connotations with Spencer's *The Faerie Queen*. Such is the fiction that has attracted both mother and daughter. An audience, lacking a text, would be ignorant of this description, although many of Sergius' subsequent physical actions (as when he *'posts himself with conscious dignity against the rail of the steps'* II, 284–5) are designed to reinforce the impression visually.[52]

This 'superb' Sergius, 'improved' by the 'campaign', the embodiment of military glory, proves a walking paradox: he 'won the battle the wrong way when our worthy Russian generals were losing it the right way' (II, 287–96). The Shavian attack on warfare is palpable since commonsense dictates Sergius' cavalry charge against gun emplacements was stupid. However, although Shaw refers to the Battle of Slivnitza, his Victorian audience would associate the charge instinctively with that of the Light Brigade at the Battle of Balaclava (25 October 1854) which was forever imprinted on English memory through Tennyson's 1854 eponymous poem. Again reality is transmuted through fiction.

Sergius displays an absoluteness that is captured in his 'I never withdraw' (II, 313). By mechanical repetition of the phrase (originally spoken by a contemporary, R.B. Cunninghame-Graham), Shaw inverts reality and reduces Sergius to a farcical stage device. Raina's entrance reinforces this mechanistic aspect:

> *She makes a charming picture as they turn to look at her. She wears an underdress of pale green silk, draped with an overdress of thin ecru canvas embroidered with gold. She is crowned with a dainty eastern cap of gold tinsel.* SERGIUS *goes impulsively to meet her. Posing regally, she presents her hand: he drops chivalrously on one knee and kisses it.*

PETKOFF [*aside to* CATHERINE, *beaming with parental pride*]
Pretty, isnt it? She always appears at the right moment.
CATHERINE [*impatiently*]

---

52 These extensive descriptions are also absent from the early scripts, although presumably Shaw would have attempted to convey his concept of the characters to the actors involved.

Yes: she listens for it. It is an abominable habit.

SERGIUS *leads* RAINA *forward with splendid gallantry. When they arrive at the table, she turns to him with a bend of the head: he bows; and thus they separate, he coming to his place, and she going behind her father's chair.*

(II, 323–36)

Here is the stately entrance, a stage tableau, a formalized procession with every rehearsed movement and gesture far removed from the reality of the (off-stage) battlefield background.

Further examples of the fictionalised Sergius abound. The 'higher love' duologue becomes an unsung operatic duet, evoking echoes of chivalric literature and Victor Hugo (II, 453–86). Sergius' seduction scene with Louka transforms him into a stereotypical nineteenth-century theatrical villain as '*He takes a stealthy look at her, and begins to twirl his moustache mischievously, with his left hand akimbo on his hip. Finally, striking the ground with his heels in something of a cavalry swagger*' (II, 497–500). Before long, Sergius shifts to intrusive third-person self-description and employs anaphora, a frequent Shakespearean rhetorical device: 'What would Sergius, the hero of Slivnitza, say if he saw me now? What would Sergius, the apostle of the higher love, say if he saw me now? What would the half dozen Sergiuses who keep popping in and out of this handsome figure of mine say if they caught us here? . . . [*speaking to himself*] Which of the six is the real man? thats the question that torments me. One of them is a hero, another a buffoon, another a humbug, another perhaps a bit of a blackguard. . . . And one, at least, is a coward: jealous, like all cowards' (II, 516–20, 575–80).[53] Shaw applies additional linguistic tricks, the style of the braggart soldier, to reinforce the point, as John A. Mills has observed: 'Other features of Sergius' mode of utterance add to its novelistic flavor. Such pseudo-poetic locutions as "You lie", "I dare marry you", "You shall wait my pleasure", and "I brook no rivals", add their trumpet note to swollen phrases like "A paltry taunt", "A hollow sham", and "huge imposture of a world" '.[54] Significantly, Louka is unimpressed by either Sergius' or Raina's theatrical posing: 'I know the difference between the sort of manner you and she put on before one another and the real manner' (II, 607–9).

53 Typical examples of Shakespearean anaphora are found in 'Othello's occupation's gone' speech (*Othello*, III.iii.342–54), or Richard II's abdication scene (*Richard II*, IV.i.204–15). Archibald Henderson noted: 'Shaw told me that *Arms and the Man* was an attempt at Hamlet in the comic spirit: Shakespeare, modified by Ibsen, and comically transfigured by Shaw' (*George Bernard Shaw: Man of the Century*, 1956, p. 539).

54 John A. Mills, *Language and Laughter: Comic Diction in the Plays of Bernard Shaw*, 1969, p. 66.

Louka's perception allies her with Bluntschli who, in Act III, exposes Raina and effects her epiphany: 'How did you find me out'. She confesses 'I've always gone on like that ... the noble attitude and the thrilling voice. . . . I did it when I was a tiny child to my nurse. *She* believed in it. I do it before my parents. *They* believe in it. I do it before Sergius. *He* believes in it' (III, 284, 296–303). In this realization of her self-imposed theatrically, Raina exemplifies the notion that spurious ideals, false ideas, and romanticism need to be stripped away in order to perceive reality, to know oneself. Yet, ironically, the consequence of Raina's realization is Bluntschli's declaration: 'I'm your infatuated admirer' (III, 317) and his confession that he possesses 'an incurably romantic disposition. I ran away from home twice when I was a boy. I went into the army instead of into my father's business. I climbed the balcony of this house when a man of sense would have dived into the nearest cellar. I came sneaking back here to have another look at the young lady when any other man of my age would have sent the coat back' (III, 1092–7). In short, Bluntschli has not advanced: he ends the play as he began it, a theatrical archetype who climbed over a balcony into Raina's room.

Sections of Act III reprise several main ideas; for example, war, romance, and social class are central to the duologue between Louka and Sergius (III, 514–637). However, Bluntschli's pronouncement, derived from many a fairy tale – 'You and he will then make it up and live happily ever after' (III, 683–4) – aptly epitomises Shaw's technique in unabashedly resolving the plot in shamelessly theatrical terms. The classic challenge to a duel is inverted humorously by Bluntschli's choice of a machine gun against Sergius' sabre, a preamble to Sergius realising that war is 'a hollow sham, like love', and 'Life's a farce' (III, 737, 763). The coat and photograph business (III, 919–40) bears the hallmark of farce or pantomime. Moreover the play is rounded out with an 'auction scene' (another Shakespearean ploy found in, for example, *The Taming of the Shrew* [Act II.i]); it is signalled by Raina's very pointed: 'I am not here to be sold to the highest bidder', even though she is (III, 1209). Through his conveniently acquired wealth, Bluntschli outbids Sergius, satisfies the Petkoffs' bourgeois instincts, secures the heroine, and solves the remaining military logistical problems. Well might Sergius finally declare rather ambiguously: 'What a man! Is he a man!' Along with the other characters, Bluntschli has been only a theatrical artifice.[55]

55 The last two sentences originally read 'What a man! What a man!'. In a first-production prompt copy, Sergius' entire final speech was deleted (presumably by the stage manager), and the production may well have concluded with Bluntschli's 'Gracious ladies – good evening' and exit (see note to III, 1232).

Arms and the Man's first audience perceived some theatrical parallels, particularly those to W.S. Gilbert, although it is a open question whether the Chinese box-within-a box effect of Shaw's fictive devices intensifies or dilutes his thematic intentions, reducing them to a mere cerebral theatrical game. Nonetheless, the fictive filters may help emphasise the unreality, the falsity of the ideals held by the play's characters and the audiences Shaw was addressing. The ultimate irony is Shaw's use of the theatre itself as a vehicle for his point of view.

The Première

In 1894 Shaw was not a big draw on the London stage: prior to *Arms and the Man* his sole theatrical credit had been *Widowers' Houses* in 1892. Moreover, on opening night, 21 April 1894, *Arms and the Man* faced stiff competition from at least twenty current productions in the West End, including *Charley's Aunt* only half-way through its four-year run, the popular musical *The Gaiety Girl*, Henry Irving in an adaptation of Goethe's *Faust*, and the sensational hit of 1893, *The Second Mrs. Tanqueray*, finishing its run on the same evening.[56] Consequently, Shaw arranged complimentary tickets for numerous friends, sympathisers, and critics (including Oscar Wilde, Henry Arthur Jones, and William Archer), although he nearly overlooked his Aunt Georgina.[57] He generated publicity by publishing a self-interview, an ebullient puff that included every aspect of the production: costumes, cast, source of the play's title, historical background, and Shaw's approach generically and thematically.[58]

The publicity yielded results, though how successfully is problematic. The Avenue Theatre held 1,200 and, full of paying customers, generated approximately £245 per night in gross receipts. On opening night, the box office collected only £44 (18% of capacity); however, that figure might translate into 400 or 500 customers occupying the cheaper pit and gallery (at two shillings and one shilling each respectively), but fewer patrons if spread across the theatre as a whole.[59] Nevertheless, the *Daily*

---

56 See J.P. Wearing, *The London Stage 1890–1899*, 1976, items 92.359, 93.271, 94.63, and 93.123.

57 *CL*, I, pp. 424–5. Other advertising appears to have been limited; *Arms and the Man* was not advertised in *The Times* until after opening night. Indeed, on 20 April the Avenue Theatre was advertised as 'to let, with possession on the 10th of May' (*Times*).

58 *Star*, 14 April 1894; rpt. in DE, pp. 473–80.

59 My conjecture for the gross receipts is based on the seating plan of the Avenue in *The Handy Handbook of London* [1903], n.p.; financial data for Shaw's plays is derived from LSE Archives Shaw/29/1. Shaw noted: 'As far as I can ascertain, the Avenue holds, when full £200 . . . and the expenses will be about £100 a night' (*CL*, I, p. 421). The seating capacity was reduced to 679 when the Avenue was reconstructed and opened as the Playhouse in 1907 (Raymond Mander and Joe Mitchenson, *The Theatres of London*, 1975, pp. 324–6). No first-night reviews intimate that the theatre was sparsely populated; presumably many complimentary tickets were given out.

Telegraph (23 April 1894) recorded that Shaw's efforts were rewarded with a 'favourably disposed' audience.

Reviewers were slightly more ambivalent about *Arms and the Man*; while the *Pall Mall Gazette* (23 April) thought 'it is worth a wilderness of average plays', most critics did not endorse the play ecstatically or unreservedly. They agreed on the play's satiric, cynical, epigrammatic, and 'clever' attributes, its whimsicality, its Gilbertian topsy-turveydom, and its propensity to burlesque other works. Several critics noted affinities with W.S. Gilbert's *Engaged* and *The Palace of Truth*, William Gillette's *Held by the Enemy*, or detected the influence of Byron or George Meredith. A representative response came from the *Daily Chronicle*:

> The purpose . . . is to burlesque the ideal of the stage, to ridicule the sentiment which refines human nature. . . . Mr. Shaw, if he had less cynicism and more sympathy, would be able to take an enviable place amongst writers for the stage, for he is a smart dealer in epigram . . . but he does not stop at the harmless humour of travesty, he is too earnest and eager to satirise and to wound.[60]

Objections were raised to what were perceived to be gibes at the British Army. The *Sketch* (25 April) remarked mildly that 'when he got on the war topic G.B.S. was perilously serious, and risked the play by uncomplimentary remarks about our soldiers'. The *Star* (27 April) was more censorious, declaring the play 'is not improved by ad captandum [meretricious] references to the British Army, and the general folly of obedience in soldiers'. Nor was Shaw's view of war approved: 'War is painted as the sordid trade of the professional butcher rather than the lofty profession of the hero and the patriot. This may be true in its way, but that way does not go very far'.[61] Equally distasteful was Shaw's 'unflattering picture of Bulgarian life and manners', which the *Daily News* (23 April) considered inappropriate:

---

60 23 April 1894. The reviewer was amongst those who connected *Arms and the Man* with *The Palace of Truth*, and Yorke Stephens (Bluntschli) reminded him of his performance in *Held by the Enemy*.

61 *Sunday Times*, 22 April 1894. The Prince of Wales (later Edward VII) and the Duke of Edinburgh attended during the run (the Prince was abroad until 30 April), and the Duke was so provoked by Shaw's views that, reportedly, he declared 'the man is mad' (A.M. Gibbs, ed., *Shaw: Interviews and Recollections*, 1990, p. 128; however, the Prince's visit was not recorded in *The Times'* Court Circulars for the period, though nine other theatre visits were). St. John Ervine's account of this event, placing it during the 1907 revival at the Savoy, is inaccurate (*Bernard Shaw: His Life, Work and Friends*, 1956, pp. 266–7), as is clear from Shaw's reference to the incident in *CL*, I, p. 631. The story, with variations, has become part of theatrical folklore.

To represent Bulgarian maidens as, without exception, liars, flirts, and hypocrites, Bulgarian heroes as adding to these qualities cowardice and braggadocio, Bulgarian officers as illiterate and incompetent, and Bulgarian folk in general as mean in mind and thought, and disgustingly filthy in their personal habits, may of course be only Mr. Shaw's fun ... it is out of place in this farcical setting.

This reviewer remarked perceptively that 'neither the battle of Slivnitza nor the treaty, though they are brought into the playbill with an emphatic display of precise dates ... [have] any necessary connection with the action'. William Archer criticized 'all this topographical pedantry' that merely emphasised the 'unreality' of the setting. It was as though Shaw had consulted two sources – one on Bulgaria, another on psychology – 'and combined the two in an essay on "Bulgarian Psychology" '.[62]

Critics were further bewildered by Shaw's dramaturgy – exactly what kind of play had he written and how? Archer was disconcerted by Shaw 'always jumping from key to key, without an attempt at modulation, and nine times out of ten he does not himself know what key he is writing in' (*World*). While the play possessed 'high qualities of frank fun, of mordant humour ... the setting of them is of the most contorted kind – half in earnest, half in levity, and with consistency only in basic pessimism'.[63] The *Star* also questioned the play's consistency, raising still relevant questions about the play's genre: 'Enormously amusing, if slightly perplexing. Not fitting exactly into any ready-made catalogue, but a nondescript, an amalgam of burlesque, farce, and comedy'. The *Daily Telegraph* was irritated by Shaw's technique of developing sympathy for his 'puppets' only to later 'cheat them of their interest'. That approach might be unconventional, but 'audiences will soon know that when the ostensible hero is introduced to them as the soul of honour and gallantry, he is in reality a despicable fool, if not a downright knave ... [and] the "unconventionality" here involved will of a surety become more conventional than conventionality itself'.

Shaw's curtain speech added to the confusion. In response to a boo-er in the audience, Shaw responded: 'My dear fellow, I am of your opinion,

---

62 The *World*, 25 April 1894; rpt. in *The Theatrical 'World' of 1894*, 1895, pp. 111–12 and T.F. Evans, *Shaw: The Critical Heritage*, 1976, p. 62. Archer also noted that 'Saranoff and Bluntschli and Raina and Louka have their prototypes, or rather their antitypes, not in the Balkan Principalities, but in that romantic valley which nestles between the cloud-capped summits of Hampstead and Sydenham'. Louis Crompton argues that the Serbo-Bulgarian war setting is vitally important (*Shaw the Dramatist: A Study of the Intellectual Background of the Major Plays*, 1971, p. 71).

63 *Stage*, 26 April 1894.

but what are we among so many?' He 'sustained his own vein of sarcasm by professing to have written a tragedy which to his surprise had been mistaken for a farcical comedy'.[64]

Although the play itself was the focus of critical attention, reviewers indicated that the 'boisterous success' that irritated Shaw 'was due in no small degree to the sympathetic spirit' of the actors, who 'played in a becoming spirit of mock solemnity'.[65] Stephens played Bluntschli 'with admirable discretion . . . his assumption of intense fatigue was painful in its realism' and he 'deserved a medal for his curious delineation of mixed cowardly and firm temperament'.[66] Bernard Gould performed Sergius 'with a mingled air of satisfaction with his own heroics and bewilderment at the unexpected consequences they entail', although one critic thought he failed to 'convey . . . the answer to the enigma of Sergius'. Yet another critic, perhaps projecting his own notions of Victorian heroism, deemed Gould was 'impressive and thoroughly manly'.[67] Despite an uneven start, Alma Murray soon found the 'right spirit', exhibiting a 'delicate perception and rare grace', that resulted in a Raina that was 'a perfectly charming little minx'.[68] While the censorious *Daily Telegraph* declared Florence Farr 'appeared to no advantage', Archer thought she 'made a memorable figure of the enigmatic Louka', and generally she was 'clever', 'just emphatic enough', and 'bright and gipsy-like'.[69] The remaining actors received less attention; Archer observed that they 'were all as good as need be' (*World*). Overall, the *Star* declared, cast and play had 'kept the whole house in a roar of perpetual laughter', but that first-night reception was not repeated subsequently.

To-day had said that *Arms and the Man* 'is a play that every intelligent playgoer should see', but predicted 'whether [Shaw] will make money with this play is doubtful'. In fact, Shaw did make money: his five-percent royalty on the gross receipts amounted to £88 9s $0^1/_2$d; however, the

---

64 See Gibbs, *Shaw: Interviews*, pp. 127–30; *Daily Chronicle*. The boo-er was R. Golding Bright who took exception to what he thought were references to the British Army; some accounts suggest more general dissent from the gallerites (*Daily Chronicle*; *Sun*, 23 April 1894). According to W.B. Yeats, a disturbance had been anticipated and 'chuckers out' had been hired 'to put out all people who make a row' (Allan Wade, ed., *The Letters of W.B. Yeats*, 1954, p. 231). Originally Shaw called the play a 'romantic comedy'; in 1907 it was an 'anti-romantic comedy'. Shaw also referred to it as 'a sermon on war', and 'a serious play' (*CL*, I, pp. 445, 660). When published, *Arms and the Man* was designated as one of the 'pleasant' plays.

65 *Daily News; The Times*, 23 April 1894.

66 *Sunday Times; To-day*, 28 April 1894.

67 *Star; Daily Telegraph; Sunday Times*.

68 *Era*, 28 April 1894; *Academy*, 30 June 1894; *Star*.

69 *Daily Telegraph; World; Star; To-day; Era*.

production was a financial disaster, and lost £4,000.[70] *Arms and the Man* ended its run on 7 July 1894 for a total of 76 performances, ostensibly a respectable figure, although 100 performances was considered the benchmark for a long run.[71] However, a closer examination of the gross box-office receipts provides a different perspective. Total receipts at the Avenue were £1768 19s 6d, an average of some £23 per performance (less than ten-per-cent of capacity). The highest average per performance was £30 in the seventh week, the lowest, £13, in the tenth (penultimate) week. Paying audiences had been scant indeed: '. . . Shaw asked me if I would go and see his first essay as a dramatist, and accordingly my wife and I attended one of the early performances of *Arms and the Man* and found the Avenue Theatre only very sparsely filled. I need not say how surprised we were to realise that here was a landmark in the history of British drama'.[72]

Shaw's Response

Shaw's curtain speech was restrained compared to his candid opinion of the première:

> I had the curious experience of witnessing an apparently insane success, with the actors and actresses almost losing their heads with the intoxication of laugh after laugh, and of going before the curtain to tremendous applause, the only person in the theatre who knew that the whole affair was a ghastly failure.[73]

It was, he noted twenty-five years later when he 'was horrified to find that the experience of 1894 was repeating itself' in a 1919 revival, 'the beginning of that detestable effect as of all the characters being so many Shaws spouting Shavianisms'.[74] The responsibility for the debacle, Shaw determined, lay not with any inherent flaws in the play, but with the cast, the public, and the critics, and he set about castigating all three.

The 1894 cast scarcely merited censure because, as Mrs Charles Calvert (Catherine Petkoff) pointed out: 'The play . . . was produced hurriedly, we were none of us too conversant with our parts, and, at

---

70 *CL*, I, p. 447. See also Shaw's comments on the run, *CL*, I, pp. 443–5.

71 All earlier sources give inaccurate figures for the run. An additional 'flying matinee' was given at Crystal Palace on 5 June; it grossed £31 15s, Shaw's royalty was £1 11s 9d. On long runs, see John Parker, ed., *Who's Who in the Theatre*, 11th edn., 1952, pp. 1805–36.

72 J.A. Fuller-Maitland, *A Door-keeper of Music*, 1929, p. 206.

73 *CL*, I, p. 462.

74 *CL*, III, p. 646. See also *Theatrics*, pp. 152–3.

times, the public failed to grasp the intensely clever things that were thrown at them'.[75] Nevertheless, Shaw scolded the cast. Alma Murray's failing was that she had lost the 'poetry . . . the tenderness – the sincerity of the noble attitude and the thrilling voice' of Raina; consequently, 'I have no reproaches deep enough for you'. Murray's fault was that she did not believe in her part, and so 'I swear I will never go to that theatre again'.[76] He also upbraided Bernard Gould, declaring that his Sergius was one of the worst performances he had ever seen. Although he expressed concern that Gould might be straining his voice, Shaw believed Gould's fault was the same as Alma Murray's: he did not believe in his role. Not surprisingly, Gould offered to withdraw from the part, which elicited a Shavian paradox: Shaw's criticism should be ignored because he knew nothing about acting.[77]

Shaw was especially ruffled by Archer's *World* review, and launched a vigorous attack in two letters, criticizing him for 'the intense unreality of your own preconceptions' that caused Archer to compare *Arms and the Man* with W.S. Gilbert's work.[78] Shaw thought, 'Gilbert is simply a para-doxically humourous cynic. He accepts the conventional ideals implicitly, but observes that people do not really live up to them'. By comparison, 'Sergius is ridiculous through the breakdown of his ideals, not odious from his falling short of them'. Shaw was stung by Archer's criticism of his character-drawing that exhibited 'a crude and contorted psychol-ogy . . . further dehumanised by Mr Shaw's peculiar habit of straining all the red corpuscles out of the blood of his personages'.[79] Shaw retorted that Archer 'ought to be ashamed of yourself for applying such a word as

75 *Sixty-Eight Years on the Stage*, 1911, p. 253. See also rehearsal details in Josephine Johnson, *Florence Farr: Bernard Shaw's 'New Woman'*, 1975, p. 62. On Shaw's rehearsal methods, see Lewis Casson, 'G.B.S. at Rehearsal', *Drama*, No. 20 (Spring 1951), 9–13, and *Shaw on Theatre*, pp. 153–9.

76 *CL*, I, p. 435. Murray replied contritely: 'I have altered one or two points I confess & generally find them go better with the audience. I suppose it is these comedy touches you object to. I will do my best to take them all out' (p. 436). Shaw was pleased with her cor-rections (pp. 437–8). In an untitled 1946 typescript, Shaw eulogized: 'But Alma Murray's combination of the provincial *ingenue* with the *poseuse* as a Viennese opera heroine was a feat of skilled acting and natural charm that has never been surpassed' (BL Add Ms 50699 ff. 144–5).

77 Shaw's correspondence with Bernard Gould is in the Burns Library Archives, Boston College (courtesy L.W. Conolly).

78 *CL*, I, pp. 425–9. Archer repeated his opinion that *Arms and the Man* was primarily a farce in the Gilbertian mould in *Study and Stage*, pp. 10–13.

79 *World*, 25 April 1894. Nevertheless, Shaw accepted Archer's invitation to write a Preface to Archer's *Theatrical 'World'*, and there Shaw deplored the current state of the theatre business and commented on Sergius' complicated and introspective psychology (pp. xvii–xxviii).

"bloodless" to a man who is bleeding from fifty wounds to his spirit', and claimed that his 'chief object . . . is to call your attention to the fact that last night, whether it leads to a commercial success or not, totally shatters your theory that I cannot write for the stage'. Archer refrained from commenting that a play without an audience is hardly a play at all. More accurately, Shaw told R. Golding Bright that his aim had been to do 'my best to put before you a true picture of what a brave soldier who knows his business really is. I heartily wish you could bring me an audience of veterans – of men who know what it is to ride a bolting horse in a charge'.[80]

Shaw decided to elaborate publicly on his assertion that *Arms and the Man* embodied 'the realities of soldiering', and the result was 'a brilliant article in next month's New Review on Arms and the Man, giving my authorities for the military realism (there is not an original notion in the whole affair from beginning to end) and stating my position as regards cynicism and all that sort of rubbish'.[81] Shaw's opinion has been embraced by critics: '. . . the most probing look at a Shaw play is Shaw's own, in this case his partly tongue-in-cheek "A Dramatic Realist to His Critics." '[82] However, what appears 'tongue-in-cheek' is an a priori refutation of Shaw's critics: scrutiny of his authorities reveals that Shaw's evidence is skewed and barely sufficient to support his propositions.

Shaw asserts initially that his perception of reality is superior to that of drama critics because they derive their conceptions solely from the theatre: 'No class is more idiotically confident of the reality of its own unreal knowledge than the literary class in general and dramatic critics in particular'.[83] By comparison, his own experiences are taken 'from real life at first hand, or from authentic documents' (p. 485); but the fallacy is self-evident because Shaw's life (of committee meetings, concert-reviewing, playwriting) was no more 'real' than that of the critics, and reading about warfare is not experience on the battlefield.

Shaw's choice of corroborating sources is selective and deceptive, notably when he cites Lord Wolseley on courage. While his two quotations from Wolseley illustrate that soldiers can exhibit bravery and cowardice, Shaw cannot resist describing Wolseley as writing 'about war with an almost schoolboyish enthusiasm' (p. 492), a description that fails

---

80 *CL*, I, p. 434.

81 *CL*, I, pp. 427, 444. The article was 'A Dramatic Realist to His Critics'.

82 Stanley Weintraub, *Bernard Shaw: A Guide to Research*, 1992, p. 65.

83 DE, p. 486. Patrick Braybrooke believed Shaw was deceived about his creation: 'Mr. Shaw has imagined what a fighting soldier is like, his imagination has produced a brilliant play founded on a brilliant misapprehension' (*The Genius of Bernard Shaw*, 1925, p. 24).

to convey a full sense of the man's complexity. Wolseley possessed the Byronic bravery with which Shaw invests Sergius: he was wounded several times, and lost the sight of his left eye in battle. True, he could write that 'man shooting is the finest sport of all',[84] but he was so popular that, when George Grossmith performed Major-General Stanley in *The Pirates of Penzance*, Grossmith based his makeup on Wolseley.[85] He also inspired the contemporary catch-phrase 'All Sir Garnet', meaning everything is very satisfactory. Wolseley's abilities embraced the utilitarian aspects of soldiering; he concentrated on military logistics and reforms, was concerned with the welfare of soldiers (as evidenced by his *Soldier's Pocket Book*, 1869), and was mindful that battles were won by adequate equipment and supply lines. Indeed, the Wolseley reality was a fusion of the characteristics of Sergius *and* Bluntschli – idealistic hero and pragmatist – whereas Shaw portrays two distinct entities. Shaw endeavours to tip the scales against Wolseley by favouring General Horace Porter, who is 'a cooler writer than our General [Wolseley], having evidently been trained in the world, and not in the army' (p. 493). Thus, Wolseley is dismissed in the same terms as drama critics. Ironically, Porter reinforces his arguments with several literary references and anecdotes, and his experiences related in his article were not significantly different from Wolseley's.

Other sources Shaw disparages include pictures by Elizabeth Thompson (Lady Butler) and Tennyson's poem, 'Charge of the Light Brigade' (p. 498). Both are scorned by associating them with critics who have been 'trained in warfare by repeated contemplation of the reproduction of Miss Elizabeth Thompson's pictures in the Regent Street shop windows, not to mention the recitations of Tennyson's "Charge of the Light Brigade." '[86] However, Thompson's 'Calling the Roll after an Engagement, Crimea' (1874), 'Rorke's Drift' (1880), or 'Floreat Etona' (1882) portray grimly realistic aspects of warfare. For example, 'Calling the Roll' depicts a wounded or dying soldier lying in the snow, having fallen out of a line of many other wounded soldiers. Contemporaries were impressed by Thompson's 'unprecedented sympathy for the suffering and heroism of the ordinary British soldier which they [the pictures] seemed to display, a quality which was deemed especially remarkable because she

---

84 Joseph H. Lehmann, *The Model Major-General: A Biography of Field Marshall Lord Wolseley*, 1964, p. 30.

85 Whether Wolseley inspired Gilbert in writing the character has been debated: see Michael Ainger, *Gilbert and Sullivan: A Dual Biography*, 2002, p. 182.

86 p. 498. Shaw further criticized Thompson in a letter to Archer (*CL*, I, p. 429). See also Tennyson's lesser known 'The Charge of the Heavy Brigade at Balaclava', and 'Prologue to General Hamley' (which mentions Wolseley).

had never witnessed war at first hand'.[87] Although Tennyson's poem is remembered for its heroic viewpoint, its underlying premise is that 'Some one had blunder'd'; a misinterpretation of orders resulted in the charge of the Light Brigade and numerous deaths.

More convincing is Shaw's citation of Alexander William Kinglake's massive study, *The Invasion of the Crimea*,[88] which results in some irrefutable points: 'A cavalry charge attains its maximum effect only when it strikes the enemy solid' (p. 499). However, Shaw muddles Lord Cardigan's conduct whilst leading the charge. Rather than charging 'the centre gun of the battery just like a dramatic critic', Cardigan was swept along by the charge, and was forced to make a swift retreat when he found himself alone facing 'a mass of Russian cavalry', a retreat Shaw approves because Cardigan 'flinched from the first-night's ideal' of 'the stage hero' (p. 500). In fact, Cardigan was hardly a model officer: he had 'no experience of active service' prior to the Crimean war, and was more interested in regimental sartorial elegance than the practical matters of soldiering.[89] In moving the brigade forward, Cardigan adhered rigidly to standard military practice that prescribed an orderly increase in speed leading up to a full galloping charge. However, on this occasion, the heroic 'dramatic-critical formula' to charge (which Shaw ridicules) was both instinctive and rational:

> Thus when Captain White, of the 17th Lancers (who commanded the squadron of direction), became 'anxious', as he frankly expressed, 'to get out of such murderous fire [i.e. crossfire], and into the guns [the object of the charge], as being the best of two evils', and endeavouring, with that view, to 'force the pace', pressed forward so much as to be almost alongside the chief's bridle-arm, Lord Cardigan checked this impatience by laying his sword across the Captain's breast, telling him at the same time not to try to force the pace, and not to be riding before the leader of the brigade'.[90]

During the eight minute charge, the brigade sped up. Consequently, there were fewer British casualties because the enemy cannons took a considerable time to reload, and so the breakneck charge actually reduced the

87 *Oxford Dictionary of National Biography*, vol. 9, 2004, pp. 131–2.

88 *The Invasion of the Crimea: Its Origin, and an Account of Its Progress Down to the Death of Lord Raglan*, vol. 4, 1868.

89 'James Thomas Brudenell, 7th Earl of Cardigan', *Oxford Dictionary of National Biography*, vol. 8, 2004, p. 345.

90 Kinglake, p. 266.

length of lethal exposure.[91] Thus White, the practical, experienced soldier, helped to reduce casualties, whereas Cardigan's insistence on 'proper form' and 'holding back' was illogical in the circumstances: 'Even at the cost of sacrificing military order, for the moment, it was seemingly wise, after all, in the straits to which our squadrons had been brought, to let every man close upon the battery with all the speed he could gather'.[92] Accordingly, Kinglake does not validate Bluntschli's description of the calvary man as 'the poor devil pulling at his horse' in a charge (I, 495), an action that, at Balaclava, would have increased the havoc.

So, while it is true that in *Arms and the Man* Shaw corroborates that 'a battlefield [is] a very busy and very dangerous place', his assertion that 'I perverted nothing' is not inaccurate. Nor is his discovery of 'drama in real life'.

Stage History

Arms and the Man remains one of Shaw's most popular plays, although it has undergone financial vicissitudes.[93] Immediately after the London première, A.E. Drinkwater undertook an (unprofitable) British provincial tour from 3 September 1894 to 13 July 1895. His company gave 176 performances at 37 venues as far apart as Plymouth, Harrogate, and Belfast. Drinkwater recorded that 'audiences in the country were then hardly ready to do justice to Mr. Shaw' and that they could be 'absolutely unresponsive'.[94] More rewarding was Richard Mansfield's New York production (Herald Square Theatre, 17 September 1894). Shaw endeavoured to persuade Mansfield to play Sergius rather than Bluntschli: 'All Sergius's scenes are horribly unsafe in second rate hands, whereas Bluntschli and

---

91 See Mark Adkin, *The Charge: The Real Reason Why the Light Brigade Was Lost*, 2004, *passim*. Although considerable, the number of casualties was less than is popularly supposed: 'Of the 673 men and horses that started out, 113 men and 475 horses were killed, 247 men and 42 horses badly injured' (*Oxford Dictionary of National Biography*, vol. 8, p. 345).

92 Kinglake, p. 269

93 This survey focusses on major professional productions in London and New York. Information on some world-wide productions can be found in Archibald Henderson, *Man of the Century*, pp. 903–44, and Donald C. Haberman, ed., *G.B. Shaw: An Annotated Bibliography of Writings About Him: Volume III: 1957–78*, 1986. See also Samuel A. Weiss, 'Shaw, *Arms and the Man*, and the Bulgarians', *SHAW: The Annual of Bernard Shaw Studies*, 10 (1990), 27–44, Paulina Kupisz, 'The Reception of Bernard Shaw in Poland', *Shavian*, 10:3 (2006), 16–22, Michel Pharand, op. cit., *passim*, and Wendy Chen, *The Reception of George Bernard Shaw in China, 1918–1996*, 2002.

94 Henderson, *Man of the Century*, pp. 949–50. Receipts for the tour averaged £8 10s per performance, although the final nine performances at the Aquarium, Brighton, netted only £17 3s 6d (LSE Archives Shaw/29/1). See also John Drinkwater, *Inheritance*, 1931, pp. 164–6, and *CL*, I, pp. 542, 547–8, and 554, on Drinkwater's financial woes.

Raina *cannot* fail'.[95] Mansfield opted for safety and gained accolades for his Bluntschli; he possessed the 'wonderful knack of always remaining in the role even when he steps before the curtain and delivers a few words', and depicted 'the character without a superfluous tone or gesture. It is exquisite dramatic art'.[96] Nevertheless, the same reviews echoed the criticisms raised in London – the play's Gilbertisms, Shaw being too clever, gibes at Bulgarian hygiene, and a lack of sympathetic characters. The final verdict was that Shaw's 'sole object is to amuse the clever, cynical portion of his audience'.[97]

By the time *Arms and the Man* was revived in London at the Savoy Theatre on 30 December 1907, Shaw was no longer the neophyte dramatist of 1894. He thought the production had 'a very strong cast' with Robert Loraine (Bluntschli), Harley Granville-Barker (Sergius) and Lillah McCarthy (Raina),[98] while audiences had become familiar with Shaw's 'ideas and his general attitude. All is as plain to us now as ABC'.[99] Max Beerbohm was more blunt: 'Fourteen years ago he was not so far ahead in form, as he was in matter, of the average playwright. In form, indeed, he was merely abreast of the time. ... How strange and rickety that form seems now!'[100] *The Times* took issue with Shaw's conception of his characters: although Bluntschli was 'really a delightful person ... most completely executed', Shaw failed to give 'full expression' to Sergius. Hence, Loraine 'made an excellent impression', but Granville-Barker 'seemed vague and uncertain in touch'. Moreover, the women 'are rather too authentically Shavian to be quite agreeable'.[101]

---

95 *CL*, I, p. 442, and see also Paul Wilstach, *Richard Mansfield: The Man and the Actor*, 1908, pp. 259–61.

96 *New York Herald*, 18 September 1894, *New York Times*, 23 September 1894.

97 *New York Herald*. LSE Archives Shaw/29/1 records Mansfield gave 19 performances between 17 September and 10 October 1894. *Arms and the Man* was in his repertoire during a subsequent American tour that lasted until 9 April 1895. Shaw's royalties totalled £474, and he commented 'Of course it doesn't draw; whoever supposed it would?' (*CL*, I, p. 458). When Mansfield played *Arms and the Man* in New York in April 1895, a reviewer declared 'the ironical philosopher is not, after all, of much importance in the world' (*New York Times*, 24 April 1895).

98 *CL*, II, p. 740. However, during the run, Shaw criticized McCarthy's performance for lacking 'STYLE', and Granville-Barker's for 'his farcical ecstasies & imitations of the exploded king of Portugal' (*CL*, II, pp. 755–7).

99 *Illustrated London News*, 4 January 1908.

100 *Around Theatres*, 1953, p. 493 (originally printed in the *Saturday Review*, 4 January 1908).

101 *Times*, 31 December 1907. The revival ran one performance more than the première (77 performances), but the box office receipts were much higher. Shaw, enjoying variable royalties of 7½ and 10%, netted £500, or more than fives times his 1894 royalties (LSE Archives Shaw/29/1).

Loraine took up Bluntschli again in 1919, although the First World War placed both play and man in a different context. Now a war veteran, Loraine had achieved the rank of Lieutenant-Colonel in the Royal Flying Corps, and had received two distinguished medals for his gallantry.[102] Those honours might account for Loraine's performance which 'hardly seemed to have caught the right tone' in a production that was 'terribly rough and ragged ... [and] the performers of the two characters intended by Mr. Shaw to be romantic insisted upon confusing non-romanticism with theatricality'; however, another critic thought it 'a work of art duly and completely made'.[103] Shaw was unhappy with the production because he thought it repeated the errors of 1894.[104] Loraine was equally 'unShavian' during a brief revival at the Everyman Theatre on 16 September 1926: '[Loraine as Bluntschli] lets us into all his secrets at the outset, and has an air of saying: "Come, join with me in the excellent sport of pulling the Petkoff legs!"'[105]

The Second World War saw a revival at the New Theatre (5 September 1944) with a star-studded cast that included Margaret Leighton (Raina), Sybil Thorndike (Catherine Petkoff), Joyce Redman (Louka), Nicholas Hannen (Major Petkoff), Ralph Richardson (reprising his 1931 performance of Bluntschli), and Laurence Olivier as Sergius (played by John Gielgud in 1931). Fifty years after the première, Shaw's 'youthful jibe at the warlike virtues [coincided] with the rescue of civilization by those very virtues' derided in the play, and there was a 'two-edged topicality of jokes about Balkan honour and loyalty'.[106] In 1931 Shaw had advised Richardson not to 'spend a long time with your gasps and your pauses and your lack of breath and your dizziness and your tiredness', but 'to go from line to line, quickly and swiftly, never stop the flow of the lines, never stop'; now, Richardson, with his 'idiosyncratic personality', gave a 'solid and endearing portrait' that lacked just 'the last spark of perkiness'.[107]

---

102 Loraine was cited 'for conspicuous gallantry and skill, on 26 Oct., 1915, when he attacked a German Albatross biplane, getting within fifteen yards of it. When the hostile machine dived, he dived after it and followed it from a height of 9,000 ft. to 600 ft. The enemy pilot was hit, and his camera and wireless transmitter were subsequently found to have bullet holes through them. The Albatross fell in our lines' (*Who Was Who in the Theatre: 1912–1976*, 1978, p. 1530).

103 *Athenaeum*, 26 December 1919; *The Times*, 12 December 1919.

104 See fn 74.

105 *The Times*, 17 September 1926. Apparently Loraine regarded *Arms and the Man* as something of a filler in his repertoire, and Shaw turned down his request for a 'stopgap' revival in 1929 (see *Bernard Shaw and Barry Jackson*, ed. L.W. Conolly, 2002, p. 45).

106 *The Times*, 6 September 1944. The production ran 67 performances.

107 John Miller, *Ralph Richardson: The Authorized Biography*, 1996, p. 41; Jonathan Croall, *Gielgud: A Theatrical Life*, 2001, p. 141; *The Times*.

While in 1931 Gielgud, perhaps not an obvious choice for Sergius, succeeded in conveying the 'number of souls – the heroic, the craven, the unscrupulous, the honourable, and the purely comic' that comprise Sergius,[108] Olivier 'was not at all keen to do' the part, floundering in his understanding of the character. Tyrone Guthrie told him, 'if you can't love him you'll never be any good in him', and it took Olivier a week to discover he could: 'I loved him for his faults, for his showing off, his absurdity, his bland doltishness'. Success followed: Olivier's 'tinsel *magnifico* Sergius, combines every touch of spur and moustache-twitching into a performance of the richest comedy'.[109]

Later in the twentieth century London saw regular productions of varying merit. The play enjoyed 'a pleasing revival' with a theory 'still worth considering' in 1953.[110] A novel departure was a satisfactory in-the-round presentation at Croydon in 1960 that, of necessity, placed emphasis on the text rather than the decor. Two years later the 'open stage of the Mermaid Theatre' was deemed 'resistant to comedy set in a domestic interior', and as a result, 'the minutiae of intimate comic acting' was replaced by broad, robust acting and cardboard characterisations.[111] Staging was also decisive in 1981's Lyric Theatre revival that focussed on the Victorianism of *Arms and the Man*, the stage becoming a 'toy theatre space'. Richard Briers and Peter Egan as Bluntschli and Sergius were successful in 'the central Shavian duel', although Irving Wardle maintained the play 'is a slippery piece to get hold of'.[112] Audience imagination was tested by aircraft noise, birdsong, and broad daylight in a 1986 production at the Open Air Theatre, Regent's Park, and the critics returned a mixed verdict. *Arms and the Man* 'still retains a surprisingly sparkling vitality and relevance', said one, while another found it 'hard to appreciate, now, that in its day this play was almost revolutionary in its impact', because the production generally lacked 'the kind of elegant, comic playing' that only Brian Deacon (Bluntschli) contributed.[113]

While Mansfield introduced Shaw to America, the true early champion of his work was Arnold Daly, who staged *Candida, You Never Can Tell, John Bull's Other Island,* and the controversial 1905 production of

108 *The Times,* 17 February 1931.
109 Laurence Olivier, *Confessions of an Actor,* 1982, pp. 108, 110; *The Times,* 6 September 1944.
110 *The Times,* 26 June 1953.
111 *The Times,* 21 March 1962.
112 *The Times,* 16 October 1981.
113 *London Standard,* 6 August 1986; *Daily Telegraph,* 7 August 1986; *Guardian,* 7 August 1986.

Mrs Warren's Profession that resulted in his arrest. *Arms and the Man* joined his repertoire in 1906, and he 'made a favorable impression' as Bluntschli, a role 'well within Mr. Daly's range'; he shared the warm applause with Chrystal Herne's Raina.[114] Daly repeated the role in London (Criterion, 18 May 1911) and was considered the best Bluntschli to date: 'He can listen as well as talk expressively and, what is more, can sit still expressively'.[115] Daly was still playing the role in 1915 (Garrick, New York, 3 May) when he gave an 'easy and capable performance'; although one critic thought *Arms and the Man* had 'not stood the test of time', another averred Daly 'threw a high light on Shaw's permanencies'.[116]

In 1925 at New York's Guild Theatre, the famous Alfred Lunn-Lynn Fontanne partnership produced a performance in which, surprisingly, 'beyond the bare words of the lines there seemed to be more significance than the actors expressed'.[117] By mid-century *Arms and the Man* drew some negative responses. It was seen as 'a museum piece' that had 'undoubtedly lost some of its sharpness with the increasing modern familiarity with large-scale warfare'; the production's highlight was Sam Wanamaker's 'bravura performance in the part of the attitudinizing Major Sergius'.[118]

Among recent American productions Kevin Klein's performance as Bluntschli in 1985 at the Circle in the Square, New York, stands out. Frank Rich opined that the perfect production of *Arms and the Man* would consist of Klein playing both Bluntschli and Sergius, so suited was he to both roles.[119] Rich also thought Glenne Headley (Raina) was good as an 'alternately smart and petulant schoolgirl one small step away from maturing'. Raul Julia's broad approach to Sergius succeeded: 'And trying to figure out which of his many selves he really is – hero, buffoon,

---

114 *New York Times*, 17 April, 22 April 1906. The production, which opened in Philadelphia on 9 April 1906, and the Lyric, New York, on 16 April, ran 53 performances. Receipts were $28,827.10; although Shaw's royalty is not known, he probably collected 10% (LSE Archives Shaw/29/1).

115 *The Times*, 19 May 1911. Shaw had advised Daly not to perform in London, but nevertheless sent Daly instructions on how to perform the piece, as well as chastising Margaret Halstan (Raina) because 'All the dignity and beauty and style were gone; and you were like a comic opera soubrette without any music.' Shaw concluded 'Mr Daly is neither the right actor nor the right producer for my plays' (*Theatrics*, pp. 109–13).

116 *Nation*, New York, 100 (13 May 1915), 545; *New Republic*, 3 (8 May 1915), 18.

117 *New York Times*, 15 September 1925. The production ran 180 performances. The Federal Theatre Project staged four productions in numerous American locations in the 1930s; see Michael O'Hara, '*Arms and the Man* and the Federal Theatre: Love and War in Troubled Times', *SHAW: The Annual of Bernard Shaw Studies*, 14 (1995), 145–52.

118 *New York Journal American*, 20 October 1950; *New York Post*, 20 October 1950; *New York Times*, 20 October 1950. The production at the Arena Theatre (19 October) ran 108 performances.

119 *New York Times*, 31 May 1985.

blackguard, humbug, coward – Julia makes Sergius just what Shaw said he was, a comic Hamlet'.[120] Less successful was the 'high-strung' 2000 revival directed by Roger Rees. The production at the Gramercy Theatre, New York, attempted to be 'screamingly funny' and emphasized 'the play's farcical aspects without being very funny'.[121]

Arms and the Man has also been adapted as a comic operetta and a film. As early as 1897 Shaw adamantly opposed theatre manager Henry Lowenfeld's proposal to make a musical version of the play: 'I have been all this time recovering from the shock of your proposal to make a Comic Opera of "Arms & the Man." How c^d you possibly make it more of a Comic Opera than it is at present?'[122] A decade later Shaw had not changed his opinion and dissociated himself from the musical adaptation proposed by Rudolf Bernauer and Leopold Jacobson, with music by Oscar Straus. This piece appeared first as *Der tapfere Soldat* in Vienna on 15 November 1908, and as *The Chocolate Soldier* in New York and London. While the Viennese production achieved only 62 performances, the English version was an outstanding success, running for 299 performances at the Lyric Theatre, New York, and 500 performances at the Lyric in London – a popularity never achieved by any production of *Arms and the Man*.[123]

Shaw had reservations about allowing *Arms and the Man* to be filmed: 'I have no objection on principle to be filmed; but I have to consider the effect on my ordinary theatrical business; and my general policy is to wait until I have had a revival which shelves the play for five years or so before putting it on the filmable list'.[124] When he did permit changes to the play he insisted that they be made by himself, which he proceeded to do and took some delight in certain cinematic features that expand

---

120 *Newsweek*, 10 June 1985. Glenne Headly was complimented for resembling a youthful Maggie Smith.

121 *New York Times*, 11 February 2000.

122 *CL*, I, p. 825.

123 Shaw's entanglements in 'the thrice accursed Chocolate Soldier' are recounted in *CL*, II, pp. 741–2, 768–70, 794–6, 934–45; III, p. 730; IV, pp. 236–7; *Advice to a Young Critic*, pp. 204–07; and *Theatrics*, pp. 103–04. Shaw refused to endorse the piece, removed any material taken directly from *Arms and the Man*, and rejected any financial recompense; however, he was willing to permit an acknowledgment that the first act of *Arms and the Man* had provided a suggestion for the operetta.

124 *Advice to a Young Critic*, pp. 208, when the possibility of filming *Arms and the Man* was raised in 1928. Shaw also had to be forced 'to abandon his theory that a good film is only a filmed play' (Donald P. Costello, *The Serpent's Eye: Shaw and the Cinema*, 1965, p. 24). On an undated remnant of a film scenario, Shaw wrote: 'All this is utterly wrong. It would wreck the film. It drags in everything I have left out ... The book must be followed precisely' (HRC, Shaw/Box 4.4).

upon mere theatrical possibilities.[125] However, the result was a disaster: 'no more dismal film has ever been shown to the public'.[126] The experience did not prevent Shaw from agreeing to a second attempt by film director Gabriel Pascal. Shaw wrote the scenario which included additional scenes, dialogue, and exterior scenes, but which still followed the play text closely because, Shaw wrote: 'It is a mistake to interrupt the play by changes of scene after the audience has become interested in the characters and story'.[127] He and Pascal got as far as discussing the casting and production aspects of the film, but the project eventually fell through.[128]

Notwithstanding its numerous productions, *Arms and the Man* does not occupy a central place in the Shavian canon largely because much in the play now lacks immediacy: 'Given an audience free of drastic illusions about war, "the higher love," defending one's honor, and marrying below one's station, the play becomes a straightforward (and somewhat thin) romantic comedy in the traditional vein'.[129] Without those illusions to provide a focus, one temptation in staging the play nowadays is to stress the farcical elements and to reduce the characters to caricatures. Such was the propensity of the 2006 Shaw Festival Theatre production which was described by one critic as receiving a 'goony farcical treatment'.[130] Shaw himself recognised that the play might not stand the test of time. When a 1904 revival was planned, he wrote that he 'was startled to find what flimsy, fantastic, unsafe stuff it is. . . . I think we had better rest on our 1894 laurels; for unless we could get a very brilliant cast together, the result of a revival would be general disappointment. It was the first "pleasant" play I ever wrote; and it was finished in a hurry to stop a gap for Miss Farr and the lady who was backing her at the Avenue. And it really would not stand comparison with my later plays unless the company was very fascinating'.[131]

125 See *Bernard Shaw and Gabriel Pascal*, ed. Bernard F. Dukore, 1996, p. xii, and Shaw's comments in the *Malvern Festival Book*, 1932, rpt. in *Shaw on Theatre*, pp. 212–13.

126 Allardyce Nicoll, quoted in Costello, p. 40. See also Costello, p. 154, for full details of the cast and production staff.

127 The scenario is reprinted in Costello, pp. 189–96, with Shaw's comment on p. 196.

128 See Dukore, *Bernard Shaw and Gabriel Pascal*, pp. 130–2, 134–9, 142–3, and Dukore, *The Collected Screenplays of Bernard Shaw*, 1980, pp. 119–25, 355–400. The play has been televised by the BBC in 1958, and 1989; a DVD of the latter is available currently.

129 Charles A. Carpenter, *Bernard Shaw & the Art of Destroying Ideals: The Early Plays*, 1969, p. 91.

130 *Buffalo News*, 12 May 2006. See also the *Toronto Sun*, 6 May 2006, *Ottawa Citizen*, 6 May 2006, and the *Hamilton Spectator*, 5 June 2006 for varied verdicts.

131 Letter to Alma Murray, 27 December 1904, BL Add Ms 50562, f. 34 (published in part in *CL*, II, p. 473).

Note on the Text

The copy text for this edition is that of the definitive edition (DE) published as *The Bodley Head Bernard Shaw: Collected Plays with Their Prefaces: Volume I: Plays Unpleasant and Plays Pleasant*, 1970, under the editorial supervision of Dan H. Laurence. DE represents Shaw's final text for *Arms and the Man* as he revised and published it in 1930 for the Collected Edition; 'This text was subsequently reset and issued in 1931–32 as the Standard Edition: it contained corrections but no further textual revision' (DE, p. 5).

Arms and the Man underwent considerable revision between its conception in 1893 and the final version some forty years later; its various forms show Shaw revising the play either in wholesale fashion, or just tweaking minor verbal nuances. However, an examination of crucial groupings of the play's variants reveals how the play took shape at three significant formative stages: the 1893 production, the first publication in 1898, and the final, definitive edition.

Shaw first composed *Arms and the Man* in three notebooks (MS), preserved in the British Library as Add Ms 50601A, 50601B, and 50601C (also published as *Arms and the Man: A Facsimile of the Holograph Manuscript*, Introduction by Norma Jenckes, New York and London, 1981). Even a cursory glance at MS reveals Shaw's holograph manuscript is frequently chaotic, with numerous revisions and deletions, many of a substantial nature. The play that materialized is spartan when compared with the elaborate DE; the manuscript then underwent substantial revision.

The manuscript finished, evidence suggests that Shaw had a fair copy made of it, probably a typescript; however, if made, it does not appear to have survived. This possibility is suggested by some passages that Shaw left unaltered in MS but which do not appear in the typescript copy made for and submitted to the Lord Chamberlain's office for licensing (LC).

LC is a typescript with Shaw's autograph revisions (BL, Add Ms 53546 'O'). Each act was typed individually, and stamped 'Mrs. Marshall's typewriting office, 126, Strand, 31 MAR [18]94'. It was submitted with the title 'Alps and Balkans', although at some point during the licensing process, the title was changed (not in Shaw's hand) to *Arms and the Man*. The play was issued a licence dated 'April 16 1894'.

Shaw also had additional typescripts made as rehearsal scripts, or prompt copies, for the performers and production personnel of the first production. One such typescript (CB) is held at Cornell University in the Bernard F. Burgunder Shaw Collection: MS 4617 (bound ms2). Purchased from Christie's auction house on 7 June 1990, it was, like LC, prepared by Mrs. Marshall's Office, and was used by Florence Farr (Louka) in the original production. However, Acts I and II are date-stamped 'APR 94' and vary slightly from LC. Act III bears the same date stamp ('31 Mar 94') as LC. Besides some further autograph revisions by Shaw, CB contains holographic additions in a hand other than Shaw's. Since these additions are concerned with stage business (such as the number of gun shots, lighting, or when members of the cast should be called), they may have been made by the stage manager, George R. Foss. This hand also records lines deleted or rearranged in rehearsal, and is designated CB/R.

Shaw was evidently dissatisfied with the text of the first production, and began to revise it even during the run of the play. Possibly the earliest such revision is the typescript held at the Harry Ransom Humanities Research Center at the University of Texas at Austin (TX1). The base copy (HRC, Shaw/Box 3.6) is the same as LC; however, while some of Shaw's revisions are the same as in LC, he made additional revisions that were incorporated into later typescripts.

The typescript (HL) held by the Houghton Library, Harvard University (MS Eng 1046.1), incorporates the TX1 revisions, and is one of a considerable number of typescripts duplicated at the same time (probably in June 1894) by 'Miss Wilkinson, 5, Stafford Street, Marylebone Rd N.W'.[132] (HL was numbered 'No. 14' by Shaw; 'No. 3' is in the Beinecke Library, Yale University [Gen Mss 279], and inscribed to Louis Weighton, the manager for the unsuccessful provincial tour that began on 21 August 1894.) HL is particularly significant because it was apparently the copy text for the first publication of the play in the United States: *Plays: Pleasant and Unpleasant: The Second Volume, Containing the Four Pleasant Plays*, Chicago and New York, 1898 (US). The play in US is revised and amplified, and substantially resembles DE; however, the text retains conventional punctuation (e.g., 'don't' for the Shavian 'dont'). It has also had a considerable longevity because it ceased being protected by previously prevailing American copyright laws and could therefore be reprinted without royalty payments. It is probably the text most familiar to American readers.

Simultaneously with the publication of US was the edition (with the same title) published in London by Grant Richards (GR). However, in the interim between despatching the copy text for US to America, Shaw made some further minor revisions to the copy text for GR. Thereafter,

132 Shaw referred to having new prompt copies duplicated in a 31 May 1894 letter to Bernard Gould (Burns Library Archives, Boston College).

the text of the play remained stable, although Shaw made further minor amendments for the productions he was involved in. Thus final corrections were not established until DE, some of which can be seen in a set of second page proofs with Shaw's corrections (HRC, Shaw/Box 4.1), date stamped by printers R. & R. Clark '1 Oct 1931', although Shaw himself initialled and dated his corrections 7 October 1930 (TX2).

It should be noted that the present edition makes no pretence to be a variorum edition; however, the notes to the text endeavour to demonstrate the nature of the 1894 production and the ways in which, subsequently, Shaw made substantial revisions and additions that result in the text we have today.

The texts of the play and appendices in this edition retain most of Shaw's idiosyncratic punctuation and spelling practices. Shaw preferred to use the apostrophe only when absolutely necessary (believing it to be redundant in most cases, and always typographically ugly), so he eliminated it whenever he could–e.g., *Ive, youve, thats, werent, wont*. He retained the apostrophe, however, in instances where its omission might cause confusion–e.g., *I'll, it's, he'll*. Shaw also retained a few archaic spellings (e.g., *shew* for *show*) and dropped the 'u' in 'our' spellings (e.g., *honor*).

Shaw also used spacing between letters to indicate emphasis of a word (e.g., h i s rather than *his*), reserving the use of italics for stage directions. However, this practice has caused considerable confusion over the years, since the variant spacing between letters of a word has not always been apparent to editors, typesetters, and proofreaders. Thus, different editions of any particular Shaw play provide different readings, sometimes indicating emphasis of a word, sometimes not. In order to avoid prolonging the confusion, and to restore and confirm Shaw's intentions for emphasizing words (as reflected in manuscript versions and in editions prepared under Shaw's supervision), this edition of *Arms and the Man*, in common with other Shaw plays published by Methuen/New Mermaids, uses italics in the conventional way for dramatic texts–i.e. both for stage directions and to indicate emphasis of particular words or phrases in the dialogue.

FURTHER READING

Bibliography and Reference

A.M. Gibbs, *A Bernard Shaw Chronology* (2001).

Dan H. Laurence, *Bernard Shaw: A Bibliography* (2 vols., 1983).

Raymond Mander and Joe Mitchenson, *Theatrical Companion to Shaw* (1955).

J.P. Wearing, Donald C. Haberman, and Elsie B. Adams, eds., *G.B. Shaw: An Annotated Bibliography of Writings About Him* (3 vols., Dekalb, IL., 1986–7).

Biography

A.M. Gibbs, *Bernard Shaw: A Life* (Gainesville, FL, 2005).

——, ed., *Shaw: Interviews and Recollections* (1990).

Archibald Henderson, *George Bernard Shaw: Man of the Century* (New York, 1956).

Michael Holroyd, *Bernard Shaw* (4 vols., New York, 1988–92).

Dan H. Laurence, ed. *Bernard Shaw: Collected Letters* (4 vols., 1965–88).

Collections of Criticism

T.F. Evans, ed., *Shaw: The Critical Heritage* (1976).

Christopher Innes, ed. *The Cambridge Companion to George Bernard Shaw* (1998).

R.J. Kaufmann, ed., *G.B. Shaw: A Collection of Critical Essays* (Englewood Cliffs, N.J., 1965).

Criticism

Eric Bentley, *Bernard Shaw 1856–1950* (New York, 1957).

Gordon N. Bergquist, *The Pen and the Sword: War and Peace in the Prose and Plays of Bernard Shaw* (Salzburg, 1977).

Charles A. Berst, 'Romance and Reality in *Arms and the Man*', *Modern Language Quarterly*, 27 (1966), 197–211.

Charles A. Carpenter, *Bernard Shaw & the Art of Destroying Ideals: The Early Plays* (Madison, WI, 1969).

Kwangsook Chung, 'Reading War, History, and Historicity in Shaw's *Arms and the Man*', *Journal of Modern British and American Drama* (Korea), 16:1 (2003) 55–76.

Bernard F. Dukore, ed., *Bernard Shaw's 'Arms and the Man': A Composite Production Book* (Carbondale, IL, 1982).

——. *Shaw's Theater* (Gainesville, FL, 2000).

Calvin T. Higgs, jr., 'Shaw's Use of Vergil's *Aeneid* in *Arms and the Man*', *Shaw Review*, 19 (1976), 2–16.

Julian B. Kaye, *Bernard Shaw and the Nineteenth-Century Tradition* (Norman, OK, 1958).

Declan Kiberd, *Irish Classics* (2000).

J. Scott Lee, 'Comic Unity in *Arms and the Man*', *SHAW: The Annual of Bernard Shaw Studies*, 6 (1986), 101–22.

Irving McKee, 'Bernard Shaw's Beginnings on the London Stage', *PMLA*, 74 (1959), 470–81.

Martin Meisel, *Shaw and the Nineteenth-Century Theater* (Princeton, N.J., 1963).

Margery M. Morgan, *The Shavian Playground: An Exploration of the Art of George Bernard Shaw* (1972).

Michael O'Hara, '*Arms and the Man* and the Federal Theatre: Love and War in Troubled Times', *SHAW: The Annual of Bernard Shaw Studies*, 14 (1995), 145–52.

Michael Quinn, 'Form and Intention: A Negative View of *Arms and the Man*', *Critical Quarterly*, 5 (1963), 148–54.

David K. Sauer, ' "Only a Woman" in *Arms and the Man*', *SHAW: The Annual of Bernard Shaw Studies*, 15 (1995), 151–66.

Stephen S. Stanton, 'Shaw's Debt to Scribe', *PMLA*, 76 (1961), 575–85.

Rodelle Weintraub, ' "Oh, the Dreaming, the Dreaming": *Arms and the Man*', in Susan Rusinko, *Shaw and Other Matters* (1998), pp. 31–40.

Samuel A. Weiss, 'Shaw, *Arms and the Man*, and the Bulgarians', *SHAW: The Annual of Bernard Shaw Studies*, 10 (1990), 27–44.

E.J. West, ' "Arma Virumque" Shaw Did Not Sing', *Colorado Quarterly*, 1 (1953), 267–80.

BERNARD SHAW

ARMS AND THE MAN

A Pleasant Play

THE PERSONS OF THE PLAY

[Avenue Theatre, 21 April 1894]

MAJOR PAUL PETKOFF   ⎫   *James Welch*
MAJOR SERGIUS SARANOFF ⎬ *Bulgarian Officers*   *Bernard Gould*
CAPTAIN BLUNTSCHLI [*a Swiss Officer in the*   *Yorke Stephens*
   Servian Army]
MAJOR PLECHANOFF [*a Russian Officer in the*   *A.E.W. Mason*
   Bulgarian Service]
NICOLA   *Orlando Barnett*
CATHERINE PETKOFF   *Mrs Charles Calvert*
RAINA PETKOFF   *Alma Murray*
LOUKA   *Florence Farr*

THE SCENES OF THE PLAY

The action occurs at Major Petkoff's House, in a small Bulgarian town, near the Dragoman Pass. The First Act takes place in November, 1885, immediately after the Battle of Slivnitza; the Second and Third Acts in the Forenoon and Afternoon of the 6th of March 1886, three days after the signature of the Treaty.

Act I   *Raina's Chamber*
Act II   *The Garden*
Act III   *The Library*

The Persons of the Play The first-night cast of characters and the cast-list. The description of the scenes is also taken from the first-night programme, which recorded: 'The Management are much indebted to Mr. J. SCHÖNBERG, Special War Artist to "The Illustrated London News," for valuable assistance generally rendered'. Johan Schönberg's pictures of the Serbo-Bulgarian war had appeared in the *Illustrated London News* in 1885–6.

MAJOR PAUL PETKOFF Originally 'The Father' and 'The General'; Shaw initially gave him the rank of general in MS.

MAJOR SERGIUS SARANOFF Originally a colonel in MS, Shaw decided to give him the same rank as Petkoff. In 1894 Shaw told Richard Mansfield: 'By the way, Sergius is a very improbable name for a Bulgarian: Would you like to change him to Marko?' (*CL*, I, p. 442).

CAPTAIN BLUNTSCHLI The only character known solely by his surname, which suggests his bluntness.

MAJOR PLECHANOFF Apparently known only by this name for the first production. In MS and all subsequent texts he is simply the Officer.

NICOLA Originally 'Michaeloff' in MS.

CATHERINE PETKOFF Originally 'The Mother' in MS.

RAINA PETKOFF Originally 'Juana' in MS.

LOUKA Originally 'Luga' and occasionally 'Stanca' in MS.

3

ACT I

Night: A lady's bedchamber in Bulgaria, in a small town near the Dragoman Pass, late in November in the year 1885. Through an open window with a little balcony a peak of the Balkans, wonderfully white and beautiful in the starlit snow, seems quite close at hand, though it is really miles away. The interior of the room is not like 5
anything to be seen in the west of Europe. It is half rich Bulgarian, half cheap Viennese. Above the head of the bed, which stands against a little wall cutting off the left hand corner of the room, is a painted wooden shrine, blue and gold, with an ivory image of Christ, and a light hanging before it in a pierced metal ball suspended by three 10
chains. The principal seat, placed towards the other side of the room and opposite the window, is a Turkish ottoman. The counterpane and hangings of the bed, the window curtains, the little carpet, and all the ornamental textile fabrics in the room are oriental and gorgeous; the paper on the walls is occidental and paltry. The 15
washstand, against the wall on the side nearest the ottoman and window, consists of an enamelled iron basin with a pail beneath it in a painted metal frame, and a single towel on the rail at the side. The dressing table, between the bed and the window, is a common pine table, covered with a cloth of many colors, with an expensive toilet 20
mirror on it. The door is on the side nearest the bed; and there is a chest of drawers between. This chest of drawers is also covered by a variegated native cloth; and on it there is a pile of paper backed novels, a box of chocolate creams, and a miniature easel with a large photograph of an extremely handsome officer, whose lofty bearing 25
and magnetic glance can be felt even from the portrait. The room is

---

Act I Dated 26 November 1893 and initially called Prologue in MS.

1–40 Brief s.d. in MS, LC, CB describe only the essentials of the bedroom, Raina's stargazing, and the date of the action. HL, US, GR, and DE are substantially similar; however, ll. 7–15 are ordered differently in US, which ignores Shaw's method for contractions (e.g., 'don't' for Shaw's 'dont').

2 *the Dragoman Pass* This lies northwest of Slivnitza, Bulgaria, where the decisive battle of the brief Servo-Bulgarian war (declared on 13 November 1885) was fought on 17–19 November. The Bulgarians gained the upper hand, the Serbians retreated, and a cease-fire was declared on 28 November 1885. Peace was established by the Treaty of Bucharest, signed on 3 March 1886.

7 *Viennese* Vienna was the capital of the Austrian Empire and set high-fashion trends.

12 *Turkish ottoman* Bulgaria became independent of the Ottoman Empire in 1878.

lighted by a candle on the chest of drawers, and another on the
dressing table with a box of matches beside it.

    The window is hinged doorwise and stands wide open. Outside, a
pair of wooden shutters, opening outwards, also stand open. On the   30
balcony a young lady, intensely conscious of the romantic beauty of
the night, and of the fact that her own youth and beauty are part of
it, is gazing at the snowy Balkans. She is in her nightgown, well
covered by a long mantle of furs, worth, on a moderate estimate,
about three times the furniture of her room.   35

    Her reverie is interrupted by her mother, CATHERINE PETKOFF,
a woman over forty, imperiously energetic, with magnificent black
hair and eyes, who might be a very splendid specimen of the wife of a
mountain farmer, but is determined to be a Viennese lady, and to
that end wears a fashionable tea gown on all occasions.   40

CATHERINE [*entering hastily, full of good news*]
    Raina! [*She pronounces it Rah-eena, with the stress on the ee*]
    Raina! [*She goes to the bed, expecting to find* RAINA *there*] Why,
    where –? [RAINA *looks into the room*] Heavens, child! are you
    out in the night air instead of in your bed? Youll catch your   45
    death. Louka told me you were asleep.
RAINA [*dreamily*]
    I sent her away. I wanted to be alone. The stars are so beautiful!
    What is the matter?
CATHERINE   50
    Such news! There has been a battle.
RAINA [*her eyes dilating*]
    Ah! [*She comes eagerly to* CATHERINE]
CATHERINE
    A great battle at Slivnitza! A victory! And it was won by Sergius.   55
RAINA [*with a cry of delight*]
    Ah! [*They embrace rapturously*] Oh, mother! [*Then, with*
    sudden anxiety] Is father safe?

---

    40   *tea gown* A long flowing dress worn at home for afternoon tea. Women would
        change into an evening gown for dinner, especially if going out.
41–4   CATHERINE (The Mother MS; s.d. om. MS, LC, CB)
    47   RAINA (Juana MS). *Dreamily* DE (*Coming in* MS, etc.)
48–9   *The stars . . . beautiful* (It is such a lovely night there is no fear of catching cold
        MS)
    57   *They embrace rapturously* DE (om. MS, etc.)

CATHERINE

Of course: he sends me the news. Sergius is the hero of the   60
hour, the idol of the regiment.

RAINA

Tell me, tell me. How was it! [*Ecstatically*] Oh, mother! mother!
mother! [*She pulls her mother down on the ottoman; and they
kiss one another frantically*]   65

CATHERINE [*with surging enthusiasm*]

You cant guess how splendid it is. A cavalry charge! think of
that! He defied our Russian commanders – acted without
orders – led a charge on his own responsibility – headed it
himself – was the first man to sweep through their guns. Cant   70
you see it, Raina: our gallant splendid Bulgarians with their
swords and eyes flashing, thundering down like an avalanche
and scattering the wretched Serbs and their dandified Austrian
officers like chaff. And you! you kept Sergius waiting a year
before you would be betrothed to him. Oh, if you have a drop   75
of Bulgarian blood in your veins, you will worship him when
he comes back.

RAINA

What will he care for my poor little worship after the acclamations of a whole army of heroes? But no matter: I am so happy!   80
so proud! [*She rises and walks about excitedly*] It proves that all
our ideas were real after all.

CATHERINE [*indignantly*]

Our ideas real! What do you mean?

---

61   *the idol of the regiment* The phrase evokes the title of Gaetano Donizetti's 1840
     opera, *La Fille du Régiment*, in which Marie awaits the return of Tonio (whom she
     marries).
67–8 *think of that!* (MS, LC add: 'The battle had been going on a long time when his
     regiment came up'; deleted in CB/R)
68   *Russian commanders* Inaccurate historically. Russia had acted as protector of
     Bulgaria, but opposed the nationalists' call for the reunification of the country;
     when the Bulgarian leader, Prince Alexander of Battenburg, decided to support
     the nationalist cause, Russia withdrew its senior officers.
71   *our gallant splendid Bulgarians* (those gallant splendid fellows MS, LC, CB)
73–4 *scattering . . . like chaff* (scattering the wretched Servian dandies like chaff MS, LC,
     CB, US; MS, LC, CB add: 'Who would have thought that Sergius had it in him?')
79–80 *acclamations* Shakespeare's sole use of the word is in *Coriolanus*, I.ix.50. Shaw
     appears to have also used it only once in his major plays.
84   *real* (om. MS, LC, CB)

7

RAINA   85

Our ideas of what Sergius would do. Our patriotism. Our
heroic ideals. I sometimes used to doubt whether they were
anything but dreams. Oh, what faithless little creatures girls are!
When I buckled on Sergius's sword he looked so noble: it was
treason to think of disillusion or humiliation or failure. And   90
yet – and yet – [*She sits down again suddenly*] Promise me youll
never tell him.

CATHERINE

Dont ask me for promises until I know what I'm promising.

RAINA   95

Well, it came into my head just as he was holding me in his arms
and looking into my eyes, that perhaps we only had our heroic
ideas because we are so fond of reading Byron and Pushkin, and
because we were so delighted with the opera that season at
Bucharest. Real life is so seldom like that! indeed never, as far as   100
I knew it then. [*Remorsefully*] Only think, mother: I doubted
him: I wondered whether all his heroic qualities and his soldiership might not prove mere imagination when he went into a
real battle. I had an uneasy fear that he might cut a poor figure
there beside all those clever officers from the Tsar's court.   105

CATHERINE

A poor figure! Shame on you! The Serbs have Austrian officers
who are just as clever as the Russians; but we have beaten them
in every battle for all that.

    88   *Oh, what ... girls are* (om. MS, LC, CB) Raina buckling Sergius sword recalls
         Shakespeare's *Antony and Cleopatra* (IV.iv.1–18; see Introduction, p. xxii).
97–100   *heroic ideas* Shaw wanted these two words enunciated clearly, and was similarly
         concerned about *glorious*, line 113 (Halstan). *CPB* provides several additional
         examples.
    98   *Byron and Puskin* Lord George Gordon Byron, English Romantic poet (see note to
         II, 256), and Alexander Sergeyevich Pushkin, Russian poet, who died in a duel to
         defend his wife's honour. He was exiled in 1820 for his liberal, revolutionary
         poetry.
   100   *Bucharest* Capital city of Romania. Opera was performed there from the late
         eighteenth-century onwards.
 102–3   *soldiership* (MS, LC, CB add: 'we credited him with', which provides a measure of
         dubiety Shaw removed later)
   105   *clever officers from the Tsar's court* DE (clever Russian officers MS, etc.). Tsar
         Alexander III (1845–94) reigned 1881–94.
   107   *A poor figure!* (And that perhaps my enthusiasms were operatic too MS, LC, CB).
         Serbs DE (Servians, throughout MS, etc.)

RAINA [*laughing and snuggling against her mother*]   110
Yes: I was only a prosaic little coward. Oh, to think that it was
all true! that Sergius is just as splendid and noble as he looks!
that the world is really a glorious world for women who can see
its glory and men who can act its romance! What happiness!
what unspeakable fulfilment!   115

They are interrupted by the entry of LOUKA, *a handsome,
proud girl in a pretty Bulgarian peasant's dress with double apron,
so defiant that her servility to* RAINA *is almost insolent. She is
afraid of* CATHERINE, *but even with her goes as far as she dares.*

LOUKA   120
If you please, madam, all the windows are to be closed and
the shutters made fast. They say there may be shooting in the
streets. [RAINA *and* CATHERINE *rise together, alarmed*] The
Serbs are being chased right back through the pass; and they
say they may run into the town. Our cavalry will be after them;   125
and our people will be ready for them, you may be sure, now
theyre running away. [*She goes out on the balcony, and pulls the
outside shutters to; then steps back into the room*]

CATHERINE [*businesslike, her housekeeping instincts aroused*]
I must see that everything is made safe downstairs.   130

RAINA
I wish our people were not so cruel. What glory is there in
killing wretched fugitives?

CATHERINE
Cruel! Do you suppose they would hesitate to kill you – or   135
worse?

RAINA [*to* LOUKA]
Leave the shutters so that I can just close them if I hear any noise.

116–19   (s.d. *Enter Louka* MS, LC, CB)
119   *dares* (US, GR add: '*She is just now excited like the others; but she has no sympathy
for Raina's raptures and looks contemptuously at the ecstasies of the two before she
addresses them*)
128   *room* (MS adds: 'JUANA (*meanwhile*) I hope there will be nothing of that kind. I
wish our people were not so cruel. There is no glory in killing wretched fugitives.
I am sure Sergius would never lift his sword against a fallen foe'. US, GR add:
'RAINA I wish our people were not so cruel. What glory is there in killing wretched
fugitives?' DE moves these two sentences to ll. 132–3)
135–6   *Cruel . . . or worse?* DE (om. MS, etc.)

CATHERINE [*authoritatively, turning on her way to the door*]

    Oh no, dear: you must keep them fastened. You would be sure to   140
drop off to sleep and leave them open. Make them fast, Louka.

LOUKA

    Yes, madam. [*She fastens them*]

RAINA

    Dont be anxious about *me*. The moment I hear a shot, I shall   145
blow out the candles and roll myself up in bed with my ears
well covered.

CATHERINE

    Quite the wisest thing you can do, my love. Goodnight.

RAINA   150

    Goodnight. [*Her emotion comes back for a moment*] Wish me
joy. [*They kiss*] This is the happiest night of my life – if only
there are no fugitives.

CATHERINE

    Go to bed, dear; and dont think of them. [*She goes out*]   155

LOUKA [*secretly, to* RAINA]

    If you would like the shutters open, just give them a push like
this. [*She pushes them: they open: she pulls them to again*] One
of them ought to be bolted at the bottom; but the bolt's gone.

RAINA [*with dignity, reproving her*]   160

    Thanks, Louka; but we must do what we are told. [LOUKA
makes a grimace] Goodnight.

LOUKA [*carelessly*]

    Goodnight. [*She goes out, swaggering*]

    RAINA, *left alone, takes off her fur cloak and throws it on the*   165
*ottoman. Then she goes to the chest of drawers, and adores the
portrait there with feelings that are beyond all expression. She does
not kiss it or press it to her breast, or shew it any mark of bodily
affection; but she takes it in her hands and elevates it, like a priestess.*

RAINA [*looking up at the picture*]   170

    Oh, I shall never be unworthy of you any more, my soul's hero:
never, never, never. [*She replaces it reverently. Then she selects*

---

145   *Dont . . . me* (om. MS, LC, CB)

155   (s.d. *kisses her and exit* MS, LC, CB)

165–9 (JUANA *goes to the table; takes up the portrait; presses it to her breast* MS, LC, CB)
       Except for DE, Raina removes her cloak earlier, at line 52.

*a novel from the little pile of books. She turns over the leaves
dreamily; finds her page; turns the book inside out at it; and, with a
happy sigh, gets into bed and prepares to read herself to sleep. But
before abandoning herself to fiction, she raises her eyes once more,* 175
thinking of the blessed reality, and murmurs] My hero! my hero!

    *A distant shot breaks the quiet of the night. She starts, listening;
and two more shots, much nearer, follow, startling her so that she
scrambles out of bed, and hastily blows out the candle on the chest of
drawers. Then, putting her fingers in her ears, she runs to the dressing* 180
*table, blows out the light there, and hurries back to bed in the dark,
nothing being visible but the glimmer of the light in the pierced ball
before the image, and the starlight seen through the slits at the top of
the shutters. The firing breaks out again: there is a startling fusillade
quite close at hand. Whilst it is still echoing, the shutters disappear,* 185
*pulled open from without; and for an instant the rectangle of snowy
starlight flashes out with the figure of a man silhouetted in black
upon it. The shutters close immediately; and the room is dark again.
But the silence is now broken by the sound of panting. Then there is a
scratch and the flame of a match is seen in the middle of the room.* 190

RAINA [*crouching on the bed*]

    Who's there? [*The match is out instantly*] Who's there? Who is that?

A MAN'S VOICE [*in the darkness, subduedly, but threateningly*]

    Sh – sh! Dont call out; or youll be shot. Be good; and no harm
will happen to you. [*She is heard leaving her bed, and making for* 195
the door] Take care: it's no use trying to run away.

RAINA

    But who—

172–7   (s.d. om. MS, LC, CB) Cf. Imogen reading in bed prior to Iachimo emerging from
a trunk (*Cymbeline*, II.ii.). Shaw also directed Raina to 'eat some sweets before
business with novels', but then had to remind the actress not to speak with chocolate in her mouth (*CPB*, p. 13).

177   *My hero! my hero!* (My hero! My darling! MS, LC, CB)

178–91 s.d. in MS, LC, CB are briefer. CB/R specifies a sequence of two shots, then two
more shots, and then three shots at ll. 178, 179, and 185. For other productions,
Shaw specified difference sequences (see *CPB*, p. 13). 'Raina is never in a hurry,
never frightened after her first pop into bed after the shots, always disdainful,
patronising, superior, queening it, until her collapse. Until then it never occurs to
her for a moment to doubt her enormous moral superiority to Bluntschli, or
Sergius's superiority. She likes him as she would like a pet dog' (Shaw's 1908
advice to Lillah McCarthy as Raina, *CL*, II, p. 756).

198–9 DE (om. MS, etc.; i.e. Bluntschli's speech is uninterrupted)

THE VOICE [*warning*]　　　　　　　　　　　　　　　　　　　　　　　　200

Remember: if you raise your voice my revolver will go off.
[*Commandingly*] Strike a light and let me see you. Do you hear.
[*Another moment of silence and darkness as she retreats to the
chest of drawers. Then she lights a candle; and the mystery is at
an end. He is a man of about 35, in a deplorable plight, bespat-*　205
*tered with mud and blood and snow, his belt and the strap of his
revolver-case keeping together the torn ruins of the blue tunic of a
Serbian artillery officer. All that the candlelight and his unwashed
unkempt condition make it possible to discern is that he is of mid-
dling stature and undistinguished appearance, with strong neck*　210
*and shoulders, roundish obstinate looking head covered with short
crisp bronze curls, clear quick eyes and good brows and mouth,
hopelessly prosaic nose like that of a strong minded baby, trim
soldierlike carriage and energetic manner, and with all his wits
about him in spite of his desperate predicament: even with a sense*　215
*of the humor of it, without, however, the least intention of trifling
with it or throwing away a chance. Reckoning up what he can
guess about* RAINA: *her age, her social position, her character, and
the extent to which she is frightened, he continues, more politely
but still most determinedly*] Excuse my disturbing you; but you　220
recognize my uniform? Serb! If I'm caught I shall be killed.
[*Menacingly*] Do you understand that?

RAINA

Yes.

THE MAN　　　　　　　　　　　　　　　　　　　　　　　　　　　225

Well, I dont intend to get killed if I can help it. [*Still more
formidably*] Do you understand that? [*He locks the door quickly
but quietly*]

201　*revolver* (pistol US)

203–20　(*She goes to the table and lights a candle. He is seen standing with his back to the
door, revolver in hand. He is an officer in the Servian uniform, a young man, aged
34, badly in need of washing and brushing* MS, LC, CB) Shaw originally described
Bluntschli as between '25 & 35'. In one production Shaw thought the uniform was
'not torn enough' (*CPB*, p. 15).

212　*quick eyes* (*quick blue eyes* US, GR; an example of Shaw's occasional tendency to
add theatrically redundant detail)

222　*Menacingly* (om. MS, LC, CB; *determinedly* US)

226–7　*Still more formidably* (om. MS, LC, CB; *Still more determinedly* US)

227–8　*quickly but quietly* DE (*with a snap* MS, etc.)

RAINA [*disdainfully*]

> I suppose not. [*She draws herself up superbly, and looks him* 230
> *straight in the face, adding with cutting emphasis*] Some soldiers,
> I know, are *afraid* to die.

THE MAN [*with grim goodhumor*]

> All of them, dear lady, all of them, believe me. It is our duty to
> live as long as we can. Now, if you raise an alarm— 235

RAINA [*cutting him short*]

> You will shoot me. How do you know that *I* am afraid to die?

THE MAN [*cunningly*]

> Ah; but suppose I dont shoot you, what will happen then? A lot
> of your cavalry will burst into this pretty room of yours and 240
> slaughter me here like a pig; for I'll fight like a demon: they
> shant get *me* into the street to amuse themselves with: I know
> what they are. Are you prepared to receive that sort of company
> in your present undress? [RAINA, *suddenly conscious of her*
> *nightgown, instinctively shrinks and gathers it more closely about* 245
> *her neck. He watches her, and adds, pitilessly*] Hardly present-
> able, eh? [*She turns to the ottoman. He raises his pistol instantly,*
> *and cries*] Stop! [*She stops*] Where are you going?

RAINA [*with dignified patience*]

> Only to get my cloak. 250

THE MAN [*passing swiftly to the ottoman and snatching the cloak*]

> A good idea! I'll keep the cloak; and *youll* take care that nobody

---

232 *afraid to die* DE (afraid of death MS, etc.) Shaw advised Lillah McCarthy (Raina
in 1907): 'You are quite right about the line in the book being "Some soldiers, I
know, are afraid of death"; but the book, as usual is wrong. Better say "afraid to
die" ' (*Theatrics*, p. 87). 'If the note of melodrama is kept up too long in the first
Act, the play will go to pieces. His first laugh must come from his reply to Raina's
"Some soldiers, I know, are afraid of death"; and thereafter, whenever Raina is
melodramatic, he is terre à terre [matter of fact]' (Shaw's 'Instructions to
Producer', HRC, Shaw/Box 4.1).

235 *as we can* (MS, LC, CB add: 'and kill as many of our country's enemies as we can';
US adds 'and kill as many of the enemy as we can')

239 *Ah; but suppose* (Oh, I dont say you are – not for the world. But even suppose MS,
LC, CB)

240 *cavalry* (MS, LC, CB, US add: '– the greatest blackguards in your army –')

244–6 RAINA ... *Stop* (*She shrinks instinctively & covers her breast with her hands*) – dont
be alarmed. Its quite correct and very pretty. Do you want to have bullets flying
and blood flowing and all sorts of horrible swearing and brutality here in your
sanctuary. (*She turns to the ottoman*) Stop. MS, LC, CB)

246–7 *Hardly presentable* (It's rather scanty US)

13

comes in and sees you without it. This is a better weapon than the revolver: eh? [*He throws the pistol down on the ottoman*]

RAINA [*revolted*]   255

It is not the weapon of a gentleman!

THE MAN

It's good enough for a man with only you to stand between him and death. [*As they look at one another for a moment,* RAINA *hardly able to believe that even a Serbian officer can be so*   260 *cynically and selfishly unchivalrous, they are startled by a sharp fusillade in the street. The chill of imminent death hushes the man's voice as he adds*] Do you hear? If you are going to bring those blackguards in on me you shall receive them as you are.

Clamor and disturbance. The pursuers in the street batter at the   265 *house door, shouting* Open the door! Open the door! Wake up, will you! *A man servant's voice calls to them angrily from within. This is* Major Petkoff's house: you cant come in here; *but a renewal of the clamor, and a torrent of blows on the door, end with his letting a chain down with a clank, followed by a rush of heavy footsteps and a*   270 *din of triumphant yells, dominated at last by the voice of* CATHERINE, *indignantly addressing an officer with* What does this mean, sir? Do you know where you are? *The noise subsides suddenly.*

LOUKA [*outside, knocking at the bedroom door*]

My lady! my lady! get up quick and open the door. If you dont   275 they will break it down.

The fugitive throws up his head with the gesture of a man who sees that it is all over with him, and drops the manner he has been assuming to intimidate RAINA.

259–63   (s.d. om. MS, LC, CB) CB/R specifies two shots before 'Do you here?'; for other
         productions Shaw specified five shots (*CPB*, p. 19).
   264   *blackguards* DE (scoundrels MS, etc.)
265–323   *Clamor . . . stops, petrified* Originally a brief, less dramatic, scene in MS, LC, CB:
         (*Someone tries the door. Hurried knocking at it behind him. He starts violently away
         from it*)
         THE MAN
            Damnation! (*Draws his sword*) Quick wrap yourself up: theyre coming.
            (*Throws her the cloak*)
         JUANA (*with all her heart*)
            Oh, thank you. (*Wraps herself in it with great relief*)
         LUGA (*outside, knocking*)
            My lady, my lady. Get up, quick, & open the door.

THE MAN [*sincerely and kindly*]   280
  No use, dear: I'm done for. [*Flinging the cloak to her*] Quick!
  wrap yourself up: theyre coming.
RAINA
  Oh, thank you. [*She wraps herself up with intense relief*]
THE MAN [*between his teeth*]   285
  Dont mention it.
RAINA [*anxiously*]
  What will you do?
THE MAN [*grimly*]
  The first man in will find out. Keep out of the way; and dont   290
  look. It wont last long; but it will not be nice. [*He draws his
  sabre and faces the door, waiting*]
RAINA [*impulsively*]
  I'll help you. I'll save you.
THE MAN   295
  You cant.
RAINA
  I can. I'll hide you. [*She drags him towards the window*] Here!
  behind the curtains.
THE MAN [*yielding to her*]   300
  Theres just half a chance, if you keep your head.
RAINA [*drawing the curtain before him*]
  S-sh! [*She makes for the ottoman*]
THE MAN [*putting out his head*]
  Remember–   305
RAINA [*running back to him*]
  Yes?
THE MAN
  – nine soldiers out of ten are born fools.

> JUANA
>   Hide yourself. Oh hide yourself, quick, behind the curtain.
> THE MAN
>   If they find me I promise you a fight – a devil of a fight. (*Hides,* JUANA *opens
>   the door. Enter* LUGA, *excitedly*)
> LUGA
>   A man has been seen climbing up the waterpipe to your balcony – a Servian
>   runaway. The soldiers want to search for him. And they are so wild and
>   drunk and furious. My lady says you are to dress at once.
> CB/R records some amendments: e.g., 'Damnation' was deleted, and 'I'll help you'
> was added before 'Hide yourself'. US, GR expand some s.d. and add some dialogue
> subsequently incorporated, e.g., 'Nine soldiers out of ten are born fools' (309).

RAINA 310

Oh! [*She draws the curtain angrily before him*]

THE MAN [*looking out at the other side*]

If they find me, I promise you a fight: a devil of a fight.

She stamps at him. He disappears hastily. She takes off her
cloak, and throws it across the foot of the bed. Then, with a sleepy, 315
disturbed air, she opens the door. LOUKA *enters excitedly.*

LOUKA

One of those beasts of Serbs has been seen climbing up the
waterpipe to your balcony. Our men want to search for him;
and they are so wild and drunk and furious. [*She makes for the* 320
other side of the room to get as far from the door as possible] My
lady says you are to dress at once, and to – [*She sees the revolver*
lying on the ottoman, and stops, petrified]

RAINA [*as if annoyed at being disturbed*]

They shall not search here. Why have they been let in? 325

CATHERINE [*coming in hastily*]

Raina, darling: are you safe? Have you seen anyone or heard
anything?

RAINA

I heard the shooting. Surely the soldiers will not dare come in 330
here?

CATHERINE

I have found a Russian officer, thank Heaven: he knows Sergius.
[*Speaking through the door to someone outside*] Sir: will you
come in now. My daughter will receive you. 335

280–94 For a 1919 revival, Shaw admonished Stella Campbell (Raina): 'You forgot to ask
Bluntschli what he was going to do when he gave you the cloak; and you did not
make enough of "Oh, *thank* you" to prepare for the change of attitude towards him'
(*Theatrics*, p. 152). Shaw told Margaret Halstan: 'Let "I'll help you" come like sun-
shine through storm clouds' (Halstan). 'But if he [Bluntschli] is not careful, he may
make the audience conclude that he is a coward. He must therefore seize certain
moments to shew that he is a brave man. These moments are, first, when he gives
Raina the cloak, and prepares to fight, and, second, when he prepares to climb down
from the window later on in spite of the fusillade outside. On both these occasions
Raina saves him from the risk he is prepared to run; and it is these sincere moments
which must make the play real and sympathetic to the audience in spite of the apparent bizarrerie of its continual violations of the conventions of theatrical romance'
(Shaw's 'Instructions to Producer', HRC, Shaw/Box 4.1). TX1 s.d. reflects Bluntschli's
bravery: 'draws his sword and faces the door like a man resolved to sell his life dearly'.

322 *sees the revolver* This business is in DE only.

A young Russian officer, in Bulgarian uniform, enters, sword in hand.

OFFICER [*with soft feline politeness and stiff military carriage*]

Good evening, gracious lady. I am sorry to intrude; but there is a Serb hiding on the balcony. Will you and the gracious lady   340 your mother please to withdraw whilst we search?

RAINA [*petulantly*]

Nonsense, sir: you can see that there is no one on the balcony. [*She throws the shutters wide open and stands with her back to the curtain where the man is hidden, pointing to the moonlit*   345 *balcony. A couple of shots are fired right under the window; and a bullet shatters the glass opposite* RAINA, *who winks and gasps, but stands her ground; whilst* CATHERINE *screams, and* THE OFFICER, *with a cry of* Take care! *rushes to the balcony*]

THE OFFICER [*on the balcony, shouting savagely down to the street*]   350

Cease firing there, you fools: do you hear? Cease firing, damn you! [*He glares down for a moment; then turns to* RAINA, *trying to resume his polite manner*] Could anyone have got in without your knowledge? Were you asleep?

RAINA   355

No: I have not been to bed.

THE OFFICER [*impatiently, coming back into the room*]

Your neighbors have their heads so full of runaway Serbs that they see them everywhere. [*Politely*] Gracious lady: a thousand pardons. Goodnight. [*Military bow, which* RAINA *returns coldly.*   360 *Another to* CATHERINE, *who follows him out*]

   RAINA *closes the shutters. She turns and sees* LOUKA, *who has been watching the scene curiously.*

RAINA

Dont leave my mother, Louka, until the soldiers go away.   365

---

337   *in hand* (MS adds: '*rather confused & apologetic*')

340   *Serb* DE (fugitive MS, etc.)

342–53 *petulantly . . . manner* The scene in MS, LC, CB is shorter and less exciting, omitting the gun fire and the Officer addressing his men below, which is introduced in HL and later texts.

353–6 In III, 222–31 Raina refers to her response as a lie, although it could be regarded as technically true.

365   *until . . . go away* (whilst the soldiers are here. (*Exit* LUGA). You can come out. (*He steps out & sheaths his sword* MS) 'RAINA *listens at door for a moment*' before telling Bluntschli to come out (CB/R).

LOUKA *glances at* RAINA, *at the ottoman, at the curtain; then purses her lips secretively, laughs insolently, and goes out.* RAINA, *highly offended by this demonstration, follows her to the door, and shuts it behind her with a slam, locking it violently.* THE MAN *immediately steps out from behind the curtain, sheathing his* 370 *sabre. Then, dismissing the danger from his mind in a businesslike way, he comes affably to* RAINA.

THE MAN

A narrow shave; but a miss is as good as a mile. Dear young lady: your servant to the death. I wish for your sake I had joined the 375 Bulgarian army instead of the other one. I am not a native Serb.

RAINA [*haughtily*]

No: you are one of the Austrians who set the Serbs on to rob us of our national liberty, and who officer their army for them. We hate them! 380

THE MAN

Austrian! not I. Dont hate me, dear young lady. I am a Swiss, fighting merely as a professional soldier. I joined the Serbs because they came first on the road from Switzerland. Be generous: youve beaten us hollow. 385

RAINA

Have I not been generous?

THE MAN

Noble! Heroic! But I'm not saved yet. This particular rush will soon pass through; but the pursuit will go on all night by fits 390 and starts. I must take my chance to get off in a quiet interval. [*Pleasantly*] You dont mind my waiting just a minute or two, do you?

366–72 LOUKA ... RAINA (om. MS, LC, CB)

374 *A narrow ... a mile* Both phrases are proverbial, indicating Bluntschli has enjoyed a narrow escape; they also embody his pragmatism. MS, LC, CB omit the second phrase.

Dear young lady (brave young lady LC, CB, TX1)

376 *the other one* DE (Servian MS, etc.)

383 *professional* This word and its variants are used nine times in the play and form a leitmotif.

383–4 *the Serbs ... Switzerland* DE (Servia because it was the nearest to me MS, etc.)

RAINA [*putting on her most genteel society manner*]
    Oh, not at all. Wont you sit down?   395

THE MAN
    Thanks. [*He sits on the foot of the bed*]

      RAINA *walks with studied elegance to the ottoman and sits*
    down. Unfortunately she sits on the pistol, and jumps up with a
    shriek. THE MAN, *all nerves, shies like a frightened horse to the*   400
    other side of the room.

THE MAN [*irritably*]
    Dont frighten me like that. What is it?

RAINA
    Your revolver! It was staring that officer in the face all the time.   405
    What an escape!

THE MAN [*vexed at being unnecessarily terrified*]
    Oh, is that all?

RAINA [*staring at him rather superciliously as she conceives a poorer*
    and poorer opinion of him, and feels proportionately more and   410
    more at her ease]
    I am sorry I frightened you. [*She takes up the pistol and hands it*
    to him] Pray take it to protect yourself against me.

THE MAN [*grinning wearily at the sarcasm as he takes the pistol*]
    No use, dear young lady: theres nothing in it. It's not loaded.   415
    [*He makes a grimace at it, and drops it disparagingly into his*
    revolver case]

RAINA
    Load it by all means.

THE MAN   420
    Ive no ammunition. What use are cartridges in battle? I always
    carry chocolate instead; and I finished the last cake of that
    hours ago.

394–401 *putting on . . . the room* (Oh no. I am sorry you will have to go into danger again
      (*Motioning towards the ottoman*). Wont you sit. (*Sees pistol*) Oh! (*She starts. He*
      shies like a frightened horse) MS, LC, CB) In US, GR, Raina merely sees the pistol
      and does not sit on it. In addition to '*he shies*', CB/R records that Bluntschli '*turns*
      quickly & half draws his sword'.

  412 *pistol and* Originally Shaw added '(*Shooting in the street – he shies again*)', but
      decided against a repetition of the effect (MS).

421–3 In A.W. Pinero's farce, *Dandy Dick* (1887), Salome asks Major Tarver 'of the
      Hussars': 'But what would you do if the trumpet summoned you to battle?', to
      which he replies: 'Oh, I suppose I should pack up a few charcoal biscuits and
      toddle out, you know' (Act II).

RAINA [*outraged in her most cherished ideals of manhood*]

Chocolate! Do you stuff your pockets with *sweets* – like a   425
schoolboy – even in the field?

THE MAN [*grinning*]

Yes: isnt it contemptible? [*Hungrily*] I wish I had some now.

RAINA

Allow me. [*She sails away scornfully to the chest of drawers, and*   430
returns with the box of confectionery in her hand] I am sorry I
have eaten all except these. [*She offers him the box*]

THE MAN [*ravenously*]

Youre an angel! [*He gobbles the contents*] Creams! Delicious! [*He*
looks anxiously to see whether there are any more. There are none: 435
he can only scrape the box with his fingers and suck them. When
that nourishment is exhausted he accepts the inevitable with
pathetic goodhumor, and says, with grateful emotion] Bless you,
dear lady! You can always tell an old soldier by the inside of his
holsters and cartridge boxes. The young ones carry pistols and   440
cartridges: the old ones, grub. Thank you. [*He hands back the*
box. She snatches it contemptuously from him and throws it away.
He shies again, as if she had meant to strike him] Ugh! Dont do
things so suddenly, gracious lady. It's mean to revenge yourself
because I frightened you just now.   445

RAINA [*loftily*]

Frighten *me!* Do you know, sir, that though I am only a woman,
I think I am at heart as brave as you.

THE MAN

I should think so. You havnt been under fire for three days as I   450
have. I can stand two days without shewing it much; but no
man can stand three days: I'm as nervous as a mouse. [*He sits*
down on the ottoman, and takes his head in his hands] Would
you like to see me cry?

RAINA [*alarmed*]   455

No.

---

428   *Hungrily . . . now* (added to GR, DE)

434–7   *He looks . . . emotion* (s.d. om. MS, LC, CB) Shaw gradually included business
developed during several productions to increase the focus on the chocolate
eating as well as Raina's reactions (see *CPB*, p. 29, and Bernard F. Dukore, *Bernard*
Shaw, Director, 1971, p. 64).

441   *grub* food

442   'If you throw the box of sweets behind you instead of down the stage, it will
knock over the candles on the chest of drawers & set the scene on fire. You all but
did that yesterday' (Halstan).

THE MAN

If you would, all you have to do is to scold me just as if I were a
little boy and you my nurse. If I were in camp now, theyd play
all sorts of tricks on me.   460

RAINA [*a little moved*]

I'm sorry. I wont scold you. [*Touched by the sympathy in her tone,
he raises his head and looks gratefully at her: she immediately
draws back and says stiffly*] You must excuse me: *our* soldiers are
not like that. [*She moves away from the ottoman*]   465

THE MAN

Oh yes they are. There are only two sorts of soldiers: old ones
and young ones. Ive served fourteen years: half of your fellows
never smelt powder before. Why, how is it that youve just beaten
us? Sheer ignorance of the art of war, nothing else. [*Indignantly*] 470
I never saw anything so unprofessional.

RAINA [*ironically*]

Oh! was it unprofessional to beat you?

THE MAN

Well, come! is it professional to throw a regiment of cavalry on   475
a battery of machine guns, with the dead certainty that if the
guns go off not a horse or man will ever get within fifty yards of
the fire? I couldnt believe my eyes when I saw it.

RAINA [*eagerly turning to him, as all her enthusiasm and her
dreams of glory rush back on her*]   480

Did you see the great cavalry charge? Oh, tell me about it.
Describe it to me.

THE MAN

You never saw a cavalry charge, did you?

RAINA   485

How could I?

THE MAN

Ah, perhaps not. No: of course not! Well, it's a funny sight. It's
like slinging a handful of peas against a window pane: first one

---

462–4   (s.d. om. MS, LC, CB) *He raises his head* (holographic addition in LC, CB)
   469   *powder* gunpowder
475–505   'Some military details came from a German staff officer who had served in the
          [Franco-Prussian] war of 1870–71: the description of a calvary charge in the first
          act is his' (Samuel A. Weiss, ed., *Bernard Shaw's Letters to Siegfried Trebitsch*, 1986,
          p. 77).
   482   *Describe it to me* (I particularly want to know MS)

21

comes; then two or three close behind him; and then all the rest 490
in a lump.

RAINA [*her eyes dilating as she raises her clasped hands ecstatically*]

Yes, first One! the bravest of the brave!

THE MAN [*prosaically*]

Hm! you should see the poor devil pulling at his horse. 495

RAINA

Why should he pull at his horse?

THE MAN [*impatient of so stupid a question*]

It's running away with him, of course: do you suppose the fellow
wants to get there before the others and be killed? Then they all 500
come. You can tell the young ones by their wildness and their
slashing. The old ones come bunched up under the number one
guard: *they* know that theyre mere projectiles, and that it's no
use trying to fight. The wounds are mostly broken knees, from
the horses cannoning together. 505

RAINA

Ugh! But I dont believe the first man is a coward. I know he is a
hero!

THE MAN [*goodhumoredly*]

Thats what youd have said if youd seen the first man in the 510
charge today.

RAINA [*breathless, forgiving him everything*]

Ah, I knew it! Tell me. Tell me about *him*.

THE MAN

He did it like an operatic tenor. A regular handsome fellow, 515
with flashing eyes and lovely moustache, shouting his war-cry
and charging like Don Quixote at the windmills. We did laugh.

RAINA

You dared to laugh!

---

492 *as she raises her clasped hands ecstatically* (om. MS, LC, CB) In his article, 'A
Dramatic Realist to His Critics' (1894), Shaw replaced the entire s.d. with '*thinking
of her lover, who has just covered himself with glory in a cavalry charge*' (DE,
p. 498).

507 *know* DE (believe MS, etc.) Shaw wanted 'know' to be stressed (*CPB*, p. 33).

515 *operatic tenor* A tenor usually sings the role of the hero or lover. There are several
styles of tenor, e.g. dramatic, lyric, buffo, helden (coincidentally, *Helden* is the
German title of *Arms*).

517 *Don Quixote* the absurd, chivalric knight/hero who tilts at windmills (thinking
them to be giants) in Cervantes' *Don Quixote de la Mancha* (1605 and 1615)

517–21 *We did laugh . . . but* DE (We nearly burst with laughing at him; but MS, etc., thus
omitting Raina's speech)

THE MAN   520

Yes; but when the sergeant ran up as white as a sheet, and told
us theyd sent us the wrong ammunition, and that we couldnt
fire a round for the next ten minutes, we laughed at the other
side of our mouths. I never felt so sick in my life; though Ive
been in one or two very tight places. And I hadnt even a revolver   525
cartridge: only chocolate. We'd no bayonets: nothing. Of course,
they just cut us to bits. And there was Don Quixote flourishing
like a drum major, thinking he'd done the cleverest thing ever
known, whereas he ought to be courtmartialled for it. Of all the
fools ever let loose on a field of battle, that man must be the   530
very maddest. He and his regiment simply committed suicide;
only the pistol missed fire: thats all.

RAINA [*deeply wounded, but steadfastly loyal to her ideals*]

Indeed! Would you know him again if you ever saw him?

THE MAN   535

Shall I ever forget him!

*She again goes to the chest of drawers. He watches her with a
vague hope that she may have something more for him to eat.
She takes the portrait from its stand and brings it to him.*

RAINA   540

That is a photograph of the gentleman – the patriot and hero –
to whom I am betrothed.

---

522 *ammunition* DE (cartridges MS, etc.) DE's amendment provides a more modern
text.

529 *for it* (MS adds:
    We'll all be courtmartialled instead, over the cartridges. I never saw such a
    piece of luck in my life. I suppose your people will make Don Quixote a field
    marshall at least.
    JUANA
    You dont think he deserves it then?
    THE MAN
    Do you want my opinion as a practical soldier?
    JUANA
    Yes.
    THE MAN
    Then I think, dear lady, that of all . . .
    This passage was deleted in LC, CB, TX1.

533, 537–8 (s.d. om. MS, LC, CB, in which Raina simply hands the portrait to Bluntschli)

THE MAN [*recognizing it with a shock*]

I'm really very sorry. [*Looking at her*] Was it fair to lead me on? [*He looks at the portrait again*] Yes: thats Don Quixote: not a   545
doubt of it. [*He stifles a laugh*]

RAINA [*quickly*]

Why do you laugh?

THE MAN [*apologetic, but still greatly tickled*]

I didnt laugh, I assure you. At least I didnt mean to. But when I   550
think of him charging the windmills and imagining he was
doing the finest thing – [*He chokes with suppressed laughter*]

RAINA [*sternly*]

Give me back the portrait, sir.

THE MAN [*with sincere remorse*]   555

Of course. Certainly. I'm really very sorry. [*He hands her the
picture. She deliberately kisses it and looks him straight in the face
before returning to the chest of drawers to replace it. He follows
her, apologizing*] Perhaps I'm quite wrong, you know: no doubt
I am. Most likely he had got wind of the cartridge business   560
somehow, and knew it was a safe job.

RAINA

That is to say, he was a pretender and a coward! You did not
dare say that before.

THE MAN [*with a comic gesture of despair*]   565

It's no use, dear lady: I cant make you see it from the professional point of view. [*As he turns away to get back to the ottoman,
a couple of distant shots threaten renewed trouble*]

RAINA [*sternly, as she sees him listening to the shots*]

So much the better for you!   570

THE MAN [*turning*]

How?

RAINA

You are my enemy; and you are at my mercy. What would I do
if I were a professional soldier?   575

THE MAN

Ah, true, dear young lady: youre always right. I know how good
youve been to me: to my last hour I shall remember those three
chocolate creams. It was unsoldierly; but it was angelic.

556–7   *He hands her the picture* 'Snatch the portrait of Sergius from him when you think
    he has had as much of it as is good for him' (Halstan).
567–70   *As he turns . . . for you* (om. MS, LC, CB; RAINA. It is fortunate for you that I dont
    look at things from the professional point of view MS, LC, CB)

24

RAINA [*coldly*]   580

Thank you. And now I will do a soldierly thing. You cannot stay
here after what you have just said about my future husband;
but I will go out on the balcony and see whether it is safe for
you to climb down into the street. [*She turns to the window*]

THE MAN [*changing countenance*]   585

Down that waterpipe! Stop! Wait! I cant! I darent! The very
thought of it makes me giddy. I came up it fast enough with
death behind me. But to face it now in cold blood –! [*He sinks on
the ottoman*] It's no use: I give up: I'm beaten. Give the alarm.
[*He drops his head on his hands in the deepest dejection*]   590

RAINA [*disarmed by pity*]

Come: dont be disheartened. [*She stoops over him almost mater-
nally: he shakes his head*] Oh, you are a very poor soldier: a
chocolate cream soldier! Come, cheer up! it takes less courage
to climb down than to face capture: remember that.   595

THE MAN [*dreamily, lulled by her voice*]

No: capture only means death; and death is sleep: oh, sleep,
sleep, sleep, undisturbed sleep! Climbing down the pipe means
doing something – exerting myself – thinking! Death ten times
over first.   600

RAINA [*softly and wonderingly, catching the rhythm of his weariness*]

Are you as sleepy as that?

THE MAN

Ive not had two hours undisturbed sleep since I joined. I havnt
closed my eyes for forty-eight hours.   605

RAINA [*at her wit's end*]

But what am I to do with you?

THE MAN [*staggering up, roused by her desperation*]

Of course. I must do something. [*He shakes himself; pulls himself
together; and speaks with rallied vigor and courage*] You see, sleep   610
or no sleep, hunger or no hunger, tired or not tired, you can
always do a thing when you know it must be done. Well, that pipe

---

581–3   *You cannot . . . but* (om. MS, LC, CB)
604–5   *Ive not . . . forty-eight hours* DE (I have not had two hours undisturbed sleep for
          three months. I am on the staff: you dont know what that means. I havnt closed
          my eyes for thirty six hours MS, etc., except GR increased thirty-six to forty-eight
          hours)

25

must be got down: [*He hits himself on the chest*] do you hear that, you chocolate cream soldier? [*He turns to the window*]

RAINA [*anxiously*]   615

But if you fall?

THE MAN

I shall sleep as if the stones were a feather bed. Goodbye. [*He makes boldly for the window; and his hand is on the shutter when there is a terrible burst of firing in the street beneath*]   620

RAINA [*rushing to him*]

Stop! [*She seizes him recklessly, and pulls him quite round*] Theyll kill you.

THE MAN [*coolly, but attentively*]

Never mind: this sort of thing is all in my day's work. I'm   625
bound to take my chance. [*Decisively*] Now do what I tell you.
Put out the candle; so that they shant see the light when I open
the shutters. And keep away from the window, whatever you
do. If they see me theyre sure to have a shot at me.

RAINA [*clinging to him*]   630

Theyre sure to see you: it's bright moonlight. I'll save you. Oh,
how can you be so indifferent! You want me to save you, dont
you?

THE MAN

I really dont want to be troublesome. [*She shakes him in her*   635
impatience] I am not indifferent, dear young lady, I assure you.
But how is it to be done?

RAINA

Come away from the window. [*She takes him firmly back to the*
middle of the room. The moment she releases him he turns   640
mechanically towards the window again. She seizes him and turns
him back, exclaiming] Please! [*He becomes motionless, like a hyp-*
notized rabbit, his fatigue gaining fast on him. She releases him,
and addresses him patronizingly] Now listen. You must trust to

    613   (s.d. *to himself* MS, LC, CB)

    620–2 Shaw told Stella Campbell: 'You did not scream Stop *through* the shooting'
           (*Theatrics*, p. 152). Shaw prescribed six shots (BL Add Ms 50602).

    625   *Never mind* (MS adds: 'I suppose I ought to go instead of hiding here. Well, I
           really dont want to be troublesome'. Shaw moved the latter sentence to line 635)

    635–6 *She shakes . . . impatience* (*She releases him with a gesture signifying that he is an*
           impossible person MS, LC, CB)

    639–44 *Come away . . . listen* (om. MS; s.d. om. LC, CB; US, GR s.d.: *She coaxes him back*
           to the middle of the room. He submits humbly. She releases him, and addresses him
           patronizingly)

our hospitality. You do not yet know in whose house you are. I   645
am a Petkoff.

THE MAN

A pet what?

RAINA [*rather indignantly*]

I mean that I belong to the family of the Petkoffs, the richest   650
and best known in our country.

THE MAN

Oh yes, of course. I beg your pardon. The Petkoffs, to be sure.
How stupid of me!

RAINA   655

You know you never heard of them until this moment. How
can you stoop to pretend!

THE MAN

Forgive me: I'm too tired to think; and the change of subject
was too much for me. Dont scold me.   660

RAINA

I forgot. It might make you cry. [*He nods, quite seriously. She
pouts and then resumes her patronizing tone*] I must tell you that
my father holds the highest command of any Bulgarian in our
army. He is [*proudly*] a Major.   665

THE MAN [*pretending to be deeply impressed*]

A Major! Bless me! Think of that!

RAINA

You shewed great ignorance in thinking that it was necessary to
climb up to the balcony because ours is the only private house   670
that has two rows of windows. There is a flight of stairs inside
to get up and down by.

THE MAN

Stairs! How grand! You live in great luxury indeed, dear young
lady.   675

RAINA

Do you know what a library is?

---

648   *A pet what?* DE (Whats that? MS, etc.; i.e. no pun)

659–60   *Forgive . . . for me* (om. MS, LC, CB)

662–92   Shaw's first version (MS) was briefer, and raised the issue of Bluntschli's family
history when Raina asked him 'No doubt your own family is noble'. She greeted
the news of his father owning hotels and his grandfather being a 'goldsmith –
pawnbroker in fact' with 'marked hauteur'.

THE MAN

A library? A roomful of books?

RAINA   680

Yes. We have one, the only one in Bulgaria.

THE MAN

Actually a real library! I should like to see that.

RAINA [*affectedly*]

I tell you these things to shew you that you are not in the house   685
of ignorant country folk who would kill you the moment they
saw your Serbian uniform, but among civilized people. We go
to Bucharest every year for the opera season; and I have spent a
whole month in Vienna.

THE MAN   690

I saw that, dear young lady. I saw at once that you knew the
world.

RAINA

Have you ever seen the opera of Ernani?

THE MAN   695

Is that the one with the devil in it in red velvet, and a soldiers'
chorus?

RAINA [*contemptuously*]

No!

THE MAN [*stifling a heavy sigh of weariness*]   700

Then I dont know it.

RAINA

I thought you might have remembered the great scene where
Ernani, flying from his foes just as you are tonight, takes refuge
in the castle of his bitterest enemy, an old Castilian noble. The   705
noble refuses to give him up. His guest is sacred to him.

---

694   *Ernani* An opera by Giuseppe Verdi, first performed in 1844. A recent London
         performance was at the Shaftesbury Theatre, 22 October 1891. Act II contains the
         fugitive and hospitality motif.

696–7 *one with ... chorus* Charles Gounod's opera, *Faust* (1859); it was performed
         frequently in London in the 1890s. The soldiers' chorus, 'Gloire immortelle de nos
         aïeux' [immortal glory of our forefathers], occurs in Act IV.ii; Shaw may have
         intended a certain irony with regard to Bluntschli's own lineage.

699   Shaw thought originally to add 'That is *Faust*', but deleted the sentence (MS).

703   ' "I thought perhaps [*sic*] you might have remembered" &c – ardent dreaming'
         (Halstan).

704   *from his foes* (om. MS, LC, CB)

705   *Castilian* native of Castile, Spain

THE MAN [*quickly, waking up a little*]

Have your people got that notion?

RAINA [*with dignity*]

My mother and I can understand that notion, as you call it.   710
And if instead of threatening me with your pistol as you did
you had simply thrown yourself as a fugitive on our hospitality,
you would have been as safe as in your father's house.

THE MAN

Quite sure?   715

RAINA [*turning her back on him in disgust*]

Oh, it is useless to try to make *you* understand.

THE MAN

Dont be angry: you see how awkward it would be for me if
there was any mistake. My father is a very hospitable man: he   720
keeps six hotels; but I couldnt trust him as far as that. What
about your father?

RAINA

He is away at Slivnitza fighting for his country. I answer for
your safety. There is my hand in pledge of it. Will that reassure   725
you? [*She offers him her hand*]

THE MAN [*looking dubiously at his own hand*]

Better not touch my hand, dear young lady. I must have a wash
first.

RAINA [*touched*]   730

That is very nice of you. I see that you are a gentleman.

THE MAN [*puzzled*]

Eh?

RAINA

You must not think I am surprised. Bulgarians of really good   735
standing – people in *our* position – wash their hands nearly

---

717   'Her exclamation, "Oh, it is useless to make YOU understand," has no sense, no
      effect, unless she has been on her high horse all through' (Shaw to Lillah
      McCarthy on her 1908 performance, *CL*, II, p. 756).

724   *Slivnitza* 'SLEEVE knit, sah' was Shaw's advice on the pronunciation (Halstan).

727–38 The emphasis here on hand-washing replaced Shaw's initial dialogue about
      'soldiering is not all leading cavalry charges' (MS). Shaw's revision provides a link
      to Petkoff's remarks on personal hygiene (II, 168–82), which attracted criticism
      in 1894. After the battle of Corioli and being feted with 'acclamations hyperboli-
      cal', Coriolanus declares 'I will go wash' (*Coriolanus*, I.ix).

728–9 *I must have a wash first* (It [hand] hasnt been washed for a week MS).

29

every day. So you see I can appreciate your delicacy. You may
take my hand. [*She offers it again*]

THE MAN [*kissing it with his hands behind his back*]

Thanks, gracious young lady: I feel safe at last. And now would   740
you mind breaking the news to your mother? I had better not
stay here secretly longer than is necessary.

RAINA

If you will be so good as to keep perfectly still whilst I am away.

THE MAN   745

Certainly. [*He sits down on the ottoman*]

RAINA *goes to the bed and wraps herself in the fur cloak. His
eyes close. She goes to the door. Turning for a last look at him, she
sees that he is dropping off to sleep.*

RAINA [*at the door*]   750

You are not going asleep, are you? [*He murmurs inarticulately:
she runs to him and shakes him*] Do you hear? Wake up: you are
falling asleep.

THE MAN

Eh? Falling aslee –? Oh no: not the least in the world: I was only   755
thinking. It's all right: I'm wide awake.

RAINA [*severely*]

Will you please stand up while I am away. [*He rises reluctantly*]
All the time, mind.

THE MAN [*standing unsteadily*]   760

Certainly. Certainly: you may depend on me.

RAINA *looks doubtfully at him. He smiles weakly. She goes
reluctantly, turning again at the door, and almost catching him in
the act of yawning. She goes out.*

737-8   ' "You may take my hand". Do not forget that you are a queen condescending to
        an insect' (Halstan).

  744   *whilst I am away* (om. MS)

747–9   Shaw revised these lines several times before achieving a satisfactory result.
        Raina's 'fur cloak' was originally a 'woollen shawl', and she also slipped on 'one
        shoe' (both changed for the first production).

  762   *weakly* (*idiotically* MS, LC, CB; *foolishly* US)

THE MAN [*drowsily*]   765
   Sleep, sleep, sleep, sleep, slee – [*The words trail off into a
   murmur. He wakes again with a shock on the point of falling*]
   Where am I? Thats what I want to know: where am I? Must
   keep awake. Nothing keeps me awake except danger: remember
   that: [*intently*] danger, danger, danger, dan – [*trailing off again:*   770
   another shock] Wheres danger? Mus' find it. [*He starts off
   vaguely round the room in search of it*] What am I looking for?
   Sleep – danger – dont know. [*He stumbles against the bed*] Ah
   yes: now I know. All right now. I'm to go to bed, but not to
   sleep. Be sure not to sleep, because of danger. Not to lie down   775
   either, only sit down. [*He sits on the bed. A blissful expression
   comes into his face*] Ah! [*With a happy sigh he sinks back at full
   length; lifts his boots into the bed with a final effort; and falls fast
   asleep instantly*]
        CATHERINE *comes in, followed by* RAINA.   780
RAINA [*looking at the ottoman*]
   He's gone! I left him here.
CATHERINE
   Here! Then he must have climbed down from the–
RAINA [*seeing him*]   785
   Oh! [*She points*]
CATHERINE [*scandalized*]
   Well! [*She strides to the bed,* RAINA *following until she is oppo-
   site her on the other side*] He's fast asleep. The brute!
RAINA [*anxiously*]   790
   Sh!
CATHERINE [*shaking him*]
   Sir! [*Shaking him again, harder*] Sir!! [*Vehemently, shaking very
   hard*] Sir!!!
RAINA [*catching her arm*]   795
   Dont, mamma: the poor darling is worn out. Let him sleep.
CATHERINE [*letting him go, and turning amazed to* RAINA]
   The poor darling! Raina!!! [*She looks sternly at her daughter*]
        The man sleeps profoundly.

770–1   *trailing off . . . shock* DE (om. MS, etc.)
  780   MS, LC, CB prescribe that Catherine wears 'a handsome dressing gown'.
  796   'Be ready for Katherine [*sic*] (as far as anyone can be ready for the incalculable)
        but dont let her hurry you out of that nice baby Oo-oo-oo-oo-oo-ooooh!'
        (Halstan).
  799   MS adds: '3/12/93 (End of Prologue)' ie. finished on 3 December 1893.

ACT II

The sixth of March, 1886. In the garden of MAJOR PETKOFF'S *house.*
It is a fine spring morning: the garden looks fresh and pretty. Beyond
the paling the tops of a couple of minarets can be seen, shewing that
there is a valley there, with the little town in it. A few miles further
the Balkan mountains rise and shut in the landscape. Looking   5
towards them from within the garden, the side of the house is seen on
the left, with a garden door reached by a little flight of steps. On the
right the stable yard, with its gateway, encroaches on the garden.
There are fruit bushes along the paling and house, covered with
washing spread out to dry. A path runs by the house, and rises by two   10
steps at the corner, where it turns out of sight. In the middle, a small
table, with two bent wood chairs at it, is laid for breakfast with
Turkish coffee pot, cups, rolls, etc.; but the cups have been used and
the bread broken. There is a wooden garden seat against the wall on
the right.   15

LOUKA, *smoking a cigaret, is standing between the table*
and the house, turning her back with angry disdain on a man
servant who is lecturing her. He is a middle-aged man of cool
temperament and low but clear and keen intelligence, with the
complacency of the servant who values himself on his rank in   20
servitude, and the imperturbability of the accurate calculator who
has no illusions. He wears a white Bulgarian costume: jacket with
embroidered border, sash, wide knickerbockers, and decorated gaiters.
His head is shaved up to the crown, giving him a high Japanese
forehead. His name is NICOLA.   25

Act II MS records a false start labelled Act I which Shaw left undeleted. He then
    began with Act II.
  1 *1886* 'After much tedious negotiation, a treaty of peace between Servia and
    Bulgaria was signed at Bucharest on March 3' (*The Annual Register*, 1886, p. 372),
    and see ll. 138–9.
1–25 Brief (but not identical) s.d. merely establish the date, the garden set, and Louka
    clearing the table (MS, LC, CB). TX1 has other variant s.d. pasted over a type-
    script original.
  16 *cigaret* Louka smoking would have been regarded as an unconventional act. It
    may have been added during 1894 rehearsals. The spelling is Shaw's idiosyncratic
    preference.
  25 *NICOLA* (Michaeloff MS)

NICOLA

Be warned in time, Louka: mend your manners. I know the
mistress. She is so grand that she never dreams that any servant
could dare be disrespectful to her; but if she once suspects that
you are defying her, out you go.   30

LOUKA

I do defy her. I will defy her. What do I care for her?

NICOLA

If you quarrel with the family, I never can marry you. It's the
same as if you quarrelled with me!   35

LOUKA

You take her part against me, do you?

NICOLA [*sedately*]

I shall always be dependent on the good will of the family. When
I leave their service and start a shop in Sofia, their custom will   40
be half my capital: their bad word would ruin me.

LOUKA

You have no spirit. I should like to catch them saying a word
against me!

NICOLA [*pityingly*]   45

I should have expected more sense from you, Louka. But youre
young: youre young!

LOUKA

Yes; and you like me the better for it, dont you? But I know
some family secrets they wouldnt care to have told, young as   50
I am. Let them quarrel with me if they dare!

NICOLA [*with compassionate superiority*]

Do you know what they would do if they heard you talk like that?

LOUKA

What could they do?   55

NICOLA

Discharge you for untruthfulness. Who would believe any stories
you told after that? Who would give you another situation? Who
in this house would dare be seen speaking to you ever again?

40   *Sofia* The capital city of Bulgaria. Shaw wanted Louka to react to 'shop in Sofia' as
        though she had heard Louka's idea many times (*CPB*, p. 51).

43   *catch them saying* (see them dare say MS, LC, CB, US)

54–65 *LOUKA ... secrets* At some point during the 1894 rehearsals, these lines were
        deleted and then restored (CB/R).

33

How long would your father be left on his little farm? [*She impa-*   60
tiently throws away the end of her cigaret, and stamps on it] Child:
you dont know the power such high people have over the like of
you and me when we try to rise out of our poverty against them.
[*He goes close to her and lowers his voice*] Look at me, ten years in
their service. Do you think I know no secrets? I know things   65
about the mistress that she wouldnt have the master know for a
thousand levas. I know things about him that she wouldnt let
him hear the last of for six months if I blabbed them to her. I
know things about Raina that would break off her match with
Sergius if–   70

LOUKA [*turning on him quickly*]

How do you know? I never told you!

NICOLA [*opening his eyes cunningly*]

So thats your little secret, is it? I thought it might be something
like that. Well, you take my advice and be respectful; and make   75
the mistress feel that no matter what you know or dont know,
she can depend on you to hold your tongue and serve the family
faithfully. Thats what they like; and thats how youll make most
out of them.

LOUKA [*with searching scorn*]   80

You have the soul of a servant, Nicola.

NICOLA [*complacently*]

Yes: thats the secret of success in service.

> *A loud knocking with a whip handle on a wooden door is
> heard from the stable yard.*   85

MALE VOICE OUTSIDE

Hollo! Hollo there! Nicola!

LOUKA

Master! back from the war!

NICOLA [*quickly*]   90

My word for it, Louka, the war's over. Off with you and get
some fresh coffee. [*He runs out into the stable yard*]

LOUKA [*as she collects the coffee pot and cups on the tray, and
carries it into the house*]

Youll never put the soul of a servant into me.   95

60–1 (s.d. om. MS, LC)
   67 *levas* Bulgarian currency. 100 stotinki make one lev, plural leva (Shaw's 'levas' is
        technically incorrect).
   95 Since Louka is alone on stage, this sentence corresponds to an unrealistic brief
        soliloquy.

MAJOR PETKOFF *comes from the stable yard, followed by* NICOLA. *He is a cheerful, excitable, insignificant, unpolished man of about 50, naturally unambitious except as to his income and his importance in local society, but just now greatly pleased with the military rank which the war has thrust on him as a man of consequence in his town. The fever of plucky patriotism which the Serbian attack roused in all the Bulgarians has pulled him through the war; but he is obviously glad to be home again.* 100

PETKOFF [*pointing to the table with his whip*]

Breakfast out here, eh? 105

NICOLA.

Yes, sir. The mistress and Miss Raina have just gone in.

PETKOFF [*sitting down and taking a roll*]

Go in and say Ive come; and get me some fresh coffee.

NICOLA 110

It's coming, sir. [*He goes to the house door.* LOUKA, *with fresh coffee, a clean cup, and a brandy bottle on her tray, meets him*] Have you told the mistress?

LOUKA

Yes: she's coming. 115

NICOLA *goes into the house.* LOUKA *brings the coffee to the table.*

PETKOFF

Well: the Serbs havnt run away with you, have they?

LOUKA 120

No, sir.

PETKOFF

Thats right. Have you brought me some cognac?

LOUKA [*putting the bottle on the table*]

Here, sir. 125

PETKOFF

Thats right. [*He pours some into his coffee*]

96 *PETKOFF* (Father, and sometimes The General MS)
96–103 (*Re-enter* MICH [NICOLA] L, *following his master, a man of sixty in a military riding dress* MS, LC, CB)

CATHERINE, *who, having at this early hour made only a very perfunctory toilet, wears a Bulgarian apron over a once brilliant but now half worn-out dressing gown, and a colored handkerchief tied over her thick black hair, comes from the house with Turkish slippers on her bare feet, looking astonishingly handsome and stately under all the circumstances.* LOUKA *goes into the house.* 130

CATHERINE

My dear Paul: what a surprise for us! [*She stoops over the back of his chair to kiss him*] Have they brought you fresh coffee? 135

PETKOFF

Yes: Louka's been looking after me. The war's over. The treaty was signed three days ago at Bucharest; and the decree for our army to demobilize was issued yesterday.

CATHERINE [*springing erect, with flashing eyes*] 140

Paul: have you let the Austrians force you to make peace?

PETKOFF [*submissively*]

My dear: they didnt consult me. What could *I* do? [*She sits down and turns away from him*] But of course we saw to it that the treaty was an honorable one. It declares peace– 145

CATHERINE [*outraged*]

Peace!

128–33   CATHERINE... *circumstances* (*Enter the* MOTHER, *from the house* MS, LC, CB)
140–62   *yesterday* ... *squeeze his* 1894 version (MS, LC, CB) is much shorter with Catherine taking an acquiescent role:

    PETKOFF

    ... yesterday. Its an honorable treaty: it declares peace but not friendly relations: the two words have been expressedly struck out. If the cursed Austrians hadnt interfered we'd have annexed Servia & made Prince Alexander Emperor of the Balkans. Curse them!

    MOTHER (*Sitting down opposite him*)

    Well, never mind, dear. So glad to have you back again with me.

    FATHER

    Thank you, my love. I missed you greatly.

    MOTHER (*Affectionately*)

    Ah! (*Stretches her hand across the table to squeeze his*)

    Shaw revised these lines in HL. See also Dukore, *Director*, pp. 61–3.

146–51   The treaty declared ' "peace is restored between ... Servia and ... Bulgaria." The words "and friendly relations" followed the word "peace" in the original draft of the treaty, but they were struck out by the desire of Servia' (*Annual Register*, p. 372). Either Shaw's research was faulty, or he wished to portray Petkoff as a blustering liar in the face of his wife's assertiveness.

PETKOFF [*appeasing her*]

    —but not friendly relations: remember that. They wanted to put   150
that in; but I insisted on its being struck out. What more could
I do?

CATHERINE

    You could have annexed Serbia and made Prince Alexander
Emperor of the Balkans. Thats what I would have done.   155

PETKOFF

    I dont doubt it in the least, my dear. But I should have had to
subdue the whole Austrian Empire first; and that would have
kept me too long away from you. I missed you greatly.

CATHERINE [*relenting*]   160

    Ah! [*She stretches her hand affectionately across the table to
squeeze his*]

PETKOFF

    And how have you been, my dear?

CATHERINE   165

    Oh, my usual sore throats: thats all.

PETKOFF [*with conviction*]

    That comes from washing your neck every day. Ive often told
you so.

CATHERINE   170

    Nonsense, Paul!

PETKOFF [*over his coffee and cigaret*]

    I dont believe in going too far with these modern customs. All
this washing cant be good for the health: it's not natural. There
was an Englishman at Philippopolis who used to wet himself all   175
over with cold water every morning when he got up. Disgusting!
It all comes from the English: their climate makes them so dirty
that they have to be perpetually washing themselves. Look at
my father! he never had a bath in his life; and he lived to be
ninety-eight, the healthiest man in Bulgaria. I dont mind a good   180

---

154 *Alexander* See note to I, 68.

164 Shaw originally (MS) wrote but then deleted an additional scene in which Petkoff
and Catherine discuss Raina's future and reveal they are aware that she performs
for people. Such a scene would have anticipated the revelation made in III,
260–303 (see Appendix I).

172 *over his coffee and cigaret* (attacking the rolls MS, LC, CB, which CB/R deletes,
leaving Petkoff no business to perform in 1894)

175 *Philippopolis* modern day Plovdiv, the second largest city, located in southern
Bulgaria

wash once a week to keep up my position; but once a day is
carrying the thing to a ridiculous extreme.

CATHERINE

You are a barbarian at heart still, Paul. I hope you behaved
yourself before all those Russian officers.   185

PETKOFF

I did my best. I took care to let them know that we have a library.

CATHERINE

Ah; but you didnt tell them that we have an electric bell in it? I
have had one put up.   190

PETKOFF

Whats an electric bell?

CATHERINE

You touch a button; something tinkles in the kitchen; and then
Nicola comes up.   195

PETKOFF

Why not shout for him?

CATHERINE

Civilized people never shout for their servants. Ive learnt that
while you were away.   200

PETKOFF

Well, I'll tell you something Ive learnt too. Civilized people
dont hang out their washing to dry where visitors can see it; so
youd better have all that [*indicating the clothes on the bushes*]
put somewhere else.   205

CATHERINE

Oh, thats absurd, Paul: I dont believe really refined people
notice such things.

SERGIUS [*knocking at the stable gates*]

Gate, Nicola!   210

---

187 *my best* (MS, LC, CB add and subsequently delete: 'Civilization is all very well; but
     its possible to have too much of it. Everything in moderation')
208 *such things* (MS adds:
         . . . such things. Where is Sergius?
     PETKOFF
     He's coming presently: he'll spend the day here. He and I have no end of a
     job over this demobilising business. We've got to send the men home some-
     how. How is Juana?
     MOTHER
     Oh, Juana is always well when she chooses to be.
     PETKOFF
     Thats right. She has not been anxious or fretting about Sergius during the
     fighting, has she?

PETKOFF

Theres Sergius. [*Shouting*] Hollo, Nicola!

CATHERINE

Oh, dont shout, Paul: it really isnt nice.

PETKOFF   215

Bosh! [*He shouts louder than before*] Nicola!

NICOLA [*appearing at the house door*]

Yes, sir.

PETKOFF

Are you deaf? Dont you hear Major Saranoff knocking? Bring   220
him round this way. [*He pronounces the name with the stress on
the second syllable: Sarahnoff*]

NICOLA

Yes, major. [*He goes into the stable yard*]

PETKOFF   225

You must talk to him, my dear, until Raina takes him off our
hands. He bores my life out about our not promoting him. Over
my head, if you please.

CATHERINE

He certainly ought to be promoted when he marries Raina.   230
Besides, the country should insist on having at least one native
general.

PETKOFF

Yes; so that he could throw away whole brigades instead of
regiments. It's no use, my dear: he hasnt the slightest chance of   235
promotion until we're quite sure that the peace will be a lasting
one.

NICOLA [*at the gate, announcing*]

Major Sergius Saranoff! [*He goes into the house and returns
presently with a third chair, which he places at the table. He then*   240
withdraws]

MAJOR SERGIUS SARANOFF, *the original of the portrait
in Raina's room, is a tall romantically handsome man, with*

MOTHER

Not at all. She is too young to feel things really. Do what you can, Paul, to
hurry on their marriage: Juana is not a bit in earnest about it.

PETKOFF

Is that a reason for hurrying it on?'

The passage was then deleted in LC, CB, TX1)

242–71   (Enter NICOLA *L, followed by* SERGIUS MS, LC, CB) Shaw began substantial
expansion of his description of Sergius in HL.

the physical hardihood, the high spirit, and the susceptible
imagination of an untamed mountaineer chieftain. But his   245
remarkable personal distinction is of a characteristically civilized
type. The ridges of his eyebrows, curving with an interrogative
twist round the projections at the outer corners; his jealously
observant eye; his nose, thin, keen, and apprehensive in spite of the
pugnacious high bridge and large nostril; his assertive chin, would   250
not be out of place in a Parisian salon, shewing that the clever
imaginative barbarian has an acute critical faculty which has been
thrown into intense activity by the arrival of western civilization
in the Balkans. The result is precisely what the advent of
nineteenth century thought first produced in England: to wit,   255
Byronism. By his brooding on the perpetual failure, not only of
others, but of himself, to live up to his ideals; by his consequent
cynical scorn for humanity; by his jejune credulity as to the
absolute validity of his concepts and the unworthiness of the world
in disregarding them; by his wincings and mockeries under the   260
sting of the petty disillusions which every hour spent among men
brings to his sensitive observation, he has acquired the half tragic,
half ironic air, the mysterious moodiness, the suggestion of a
strange and terrible history that has left nothing but undying
remorse, by which Childe Harold fascinated the grandmothers of   265
his English contemporaries. It is clear that here or nowhere is
Raina's ideal hero. CATHERINE *is hardly less enthusiastic about*
him than her daughter, and much less reserved in shewing her
enthusiasm. As he enters from the stable gate, she rises effusively
to greet him. PETKOFF *is distinctly less disposed to make a*   270
fuss about him.

PETKOFF

Here already, Sergius! Glad to see you.

CATHERINE

My dear Sergius! [*She holds out both her hands*]   275

247–8   *an interrogative twist* (*a ram's horn twist* HL, US, GR)

   251   *salon* a gathering of literary or artistic figures, usually in a fashionable house

   256   *Byronism* a rejection of conventionality in all its forms as evinced in the life and
        poetry of Byron, the archetypal Romantic poet.

   265   *Childe Harold* Byron's *Childe Harold's Pilgrimage* (1812–16) describes the travels
        of the homeless, melancholic exile Harold around the Mediterranean. It was an
        immediate success on publication.

   275   (MS, LC, CB add: '*She enthusiastically embraces him and kisses him*')

SERGIUS [*kissing them with scrupulous gallantry*]

My dear mother, if I may call you so.

PETKOFF [*drily*]

Mother-in-law, Sergius: mother-in-law! Sit down; and have
some coffee.   280

SERGIUS

Thank you: none for me. [*He gets away from the table with a
certain distaste for* PETKOFF'*s enjoyment of it, and posts himself
with conscious dignity against the rail of the steps leading to the
house*]   285

CATHERINE

You look superb. The campaign has improved you, Sergius.
Everybody here is mad about you. We were all wild with enthusiasm about that magnificent cavalry charge.

SERGIUS [*with grave irony*]   290

Madam: it was the cradle and the grave of my military reputation.

CATHERINE

How so?

SERGIUS

I won the battle the wrong way when our worthy Russian gener-   295
als were losing it the right way. In short, I upset their plans, and
wounded their self-esteem. Two Cossack colonels had their
regiments routed on the most correct principles of scientific
warfare. Two major-generals got killed strictly according to military etiquette. The two colonels are now major-generals; and   300
I am still a simple major.

CATHERINE

You shall not remain so, Sergius. The women are on your side;
and they will see that justice is done you.

282–5 (s.d. om. MS; *Crosses R to steps and poses against pillar* LC) Further revisions
occurred in CB/R, indicating that Shaw's ideas on stage movement here were
refined by rehearsal.

287   *superb* DE (superb – splendid MS, etc.) The simple declarative 'superb' is more
effectively emphatic, and reinforces Catherine's enthusiasm for Sergius.

290–1 (SERGIUS. A most unlucky charge for me MS, LC, CB)

295   Originally, Sergius prefaced his speech with 'It appears it was out of the usual professional routine' (MS, LC, CB).

297   *Cossack* DE (Two of their colonels MS, etc.) Cossacks came from southern
Imperial Russian and were traditionally associated with the military, and received
tax benefits for military service.

SERGIUS 305

    It is too late. I have only waited for the peace to send in my
resignation.

PETKOFF [*dropping his cup in his amazement*]

    Your resignation!

CATHERINE 310

    Oh, you must withdraw it!

SERGIUS [*with resolute measured emphasis, folding his arms*]

    I never withdraw.

PETKOFF [*vexed*]

    Now who could have supposed you were going to do such a 315
thing?

SERGIUS [*with fire*]

    Everyone that knew me. But enough of myself and my affairs.
How is Raina; and where is Raina?

RAINA [*suddenly coming round the corner of the house and standing* 320
at the top of the steps in the path]

    Raina is here.

    She makes a charming picture as they turn to look at her. She
wears an underdress of pale green silk, draped with an overdress
of thin ecru canvas embroidered with gold. She is crowned with a 325
dainty eastern cap of gold tinsel. SERGIUS *goes impulsively to*

308–9 (PETKOFF. What! You have resigned? MS, LC, CB) Petkoff's speech was revised in
HL.

312 (*Folding his arms proudly* MS, LC, CB)

313 *I never withdraw* Spoken by R.B. Cunninghame-Graham, Liberal Member of
Parliament for Lanark N.W., during a debate in the House of Commons on 1
December 1888. A radical socialist, he had asked when there would be a debate on
the exploited chain-makers of Cradley Heath, near Birmingham. He used
'unParliamentary language', which he was asked to withdraw. He refused and was
required to withdraw from the House (*Hansard's Parliamentary Debates*, 3rd
series, vol. 331, 1888, columns 732–3). He led the 'Bloody Sunday' demonstration
against the government's Irish policy held in Trafalgar Square, London, on 13
November 1887, in which Shaw participated more discretely (see *CL*, I, pp.
177–8). Cunninghame-Graham's adventures in Morocco provided Shaw with
material for *Captain Brassbound's Conversion* (1900). Sergius is given similar
absolutist phrases throughout the play.

319 *How . . . Raina?* Cf. 'Who is Silvia? What is she' (*The Two Gentlemen of Verona*,
IV.ii.39).

meet her. Posing regally, she presents her hand: he drops
chivalrously on one knee and kisses it.

PETKOFF [*aside to* CATHERINE, *beaming with parental pride*]

Pretty, isnt it? She always appears at the right moment.   330

CATHERINE [*impatiently*]

Yes: she listens for it. It is an abominable habit.

SERGIUS *leads* RAINA *forward with splendid gallantry. When*
they arrive at the table, she turns to him with a bend of the head:
he bows; and thus they separate, he coming to his place, and she   335
going behind her father's chair.

RAINA [*stooping and kissing her father*]

Dear father! Welcome home!

PETKOFF [*patting her cheek*]

My little pet girl. [*He kisses her. She goes to the chair left by*   340
NICOLA *for* SERGIUS, *and sits down*]

CATHERINE

And so youre no longer a soldier, Sergius.

SERGIUS

I am no longer a soldier. Soldiering, my dear madam, is   345
the coward's art of attacking mercilessly when you are strong,
and keeping out of harm's way when you are weak. That is
the whole secret of successful fighting. Get your enemy at a
disadvantage; and never, on any account, fight him on equal
terms.   350

320–8 (JUANA *appears in the leafy passage, charmingly dressed*)
Juana is here.
SERGIUS
Ah! (*He goes impulsively to meet her. She stretches out her hand: he drops on*
one knee and kisses it)
MS, LC, CB)

333 *splendid gallantry* (all except DE add: *as if she were a queen*)

341 Originally Shaw added an exchange between Raina and Catherine on Sergius not
receiving due credit for his heroism, including 'JUANA If it is so terribly dangerous
to charge upon machine guns it is so much the more heroic' (MS). Shaw then
substituted and eventually deleted: '(SERGIUS *remains standing until she sits*) SERG
– No doubt it has been carefully circulated to discredit me. Well, let them. I am
glad I am no longer a soldier' (MS, LC, CB, TX1).

PETKOFF

They wouldnt let us make a fair stand-up fight of it. However, I
suppose soldiering has to be a trade like any other trade.

SERGIUS

Precisely. But I have no ambition to shine as a tradesman; so I   355
have taken the advice of that bagman of a captain that settled
the exchange of prisoners with us at Pirot, and given it up.

PETKOFF

What! that Swiss fellow? Sergius: Ive often thought of that
exchange since. He over-reached us about those horses.   360

SERGIUS

Of course he over-reached us. His father was a hotel and livery
stable keeper; and he owed his first step to his knowledge of
horse-dealing. [*With mock enthusiasm*] Ah, he was a soldier:
every inch a soldier! If only I had bought the horses for my   365
regiment instead of foolishly leading it into danger, I should
have been a field-marshal now!

CATHERINE

A Swiss? What was he doing in the Serbian army?

PETKOFF   370

A volunteer, of course: keen on picking up his profession.
[*Chuckling*] We shouldnt have been able to begin fighting if
these foreigners hadnt shewn us how to do it: we knew nothing
about it; and neither did the Serbs. Egad, there'd have been no
war without them!   375

RAINA

Are there many Swiss officers in the Serbian Army?

PETKOFF

No. All Austrians, just as our officers were all Russians. This
was the only Swiss I came across. I'll never trust a Swiss again. 380

352–5   *They . . . so I*

 (Well, Sergius, soldiering costs a great deal of money; and the nation pays us
 to win, not to shew our pluck.

 SERGIUS

 Precisely. Oh, it's a glorious trade. So I . . .

 MS, LC, CB. CB/R added: 'However I have no ambition to be a tradesman'. HL
 revises to the present text)

356   *bagman* travelling salesman

357   *Pirot* a city in eastern Serbia, north-west of Sofia

362   *hotel and* (om. MS)

374   *Egad* by God

He humbugged us into giving him fifty ablebodied men for two
hundred worn out chargers. They werent even eatable!

SERGIUS

We were two children in the hands of that consummate soldier,
Major: simply two innocent little children.   385

RAINA

What was he like?

CATHERINE

Oh, Raina, what a silly question!

SERGIUS   390

He was like a commercial traveller in uniform. Bourgeois to his
boots!

PETKOFF [*grinning*]

Sergius: tell Catherine that queer story his friend told us about
how he escaped after Slivnitza. You remember. About his being   395
hid by two women.

SERGIUS [*with bitter irony*]

Oh yes: quite a romance! He was serving in the very battery
I so unprofessionally charged. Being a thorough soldier, he ran
away like the rest of them, with our cavalry at his heels. To escape   400
their sabres he climbed a waterpipe and made his way into the
bedroom of a young Bulgarian lady. The young lady was
enchanted by his persuasive commercial traveller's manners. She
very modestly entertained him for an hour or so, and then called

---

381–2 *He humbugged . . . eatable* Substituted for a passage deleted in MS:

> JUANA
>
> What advice did he [Bluntschli] give you, Sergius?
>
> SERGIUS
>
> Oh, excellent advice. He told me I was too much of a gentleman to make a
> good officer, and suggested that I should seek adventures and write books
> about them. A cousin of his, he said, had done very well in that way.
>
> MOTHER
>
> How dared he!
>
> SERGIUS
>
> Oh, we had him to dinner, & he was very chatty & frank over it.
>
> The reference to books and adventures again associates Sergius with Cunninghame-
> Graham.

396 *hid by two women* Shaw stressed that Catherine and Raina should react to this line
(*CPB*, pp. 67, 69).

400 *rest of them* (MS, LC, CB add: 'and never stopped for breath until he arrived here',
which tends to render Bluntschli slightly more cowardly)

400–2 *To escape . . . lady* DE (To escape their attentions, he had the good taste to take
refuge in the chamber of some patriotic young Bulgarian lady MS, etc.)

403 *commercial traveller* travelling salesman (somewhat derogatory)

in her mother lest her conduct should appear unmaidenly. The   405
old lady was equally fascinated; and the fugitive was sent on his
way in the morning, disguised in an old coat belonging to the
master of the house, who was away at the war.

RAINA [*rising with marked stateliness*]

Your life in the camp has made you coarse, Sergius. I did not   410
think you would have repeated such a story before me. [*She
turns away coldly*]

CATHERINE [*also rising*]

She is right, Sergius. If such women exist, we should be spared
the knowledge of them.   415

PETKOFF

Pooh! nonsense! what does it matter?

SERGIUS [*ashamed*]

No, Petkoff: I was wrong. [*To* RAINA, *with earnest humility*]
I beg your pardon. I have behaved abominably. Forgive me,   420
Raina. [*She bows reservedly*] And you too, madam. [CATHER-
INE *bows graciously and sits down. He proceeds solemnly, again
addressing* RAINA] The glimpses I have had of the seamy side of
life during the last few months have made me cynical; but I
should not have brought my cynicism here: least of all into   425
your presence, Raina. I – [*Here, turning to the others, he is evidently going to begin a long speech when the* MAJOR *interrupts
him*]

PETKOFF

Stuff and nonsense, Sergius! Thats quite enough fuss about   430
nothing: a soldier's daughter should be able to stand up without
flinching to a little strong conversation. [*He rises*] Come: it's
time for us to get to business. We have to make up our minds
how those three regiments are to get back to Philippopolis:
theres no forage for them on the Sofia route. [*He goes towards*   435
the house] Come along. [SERGIUS *is about to follow him when*
CATHERINE *rises and intervenes*]

---

    407   *an old coat* (a cast off suit MS)
    409   *with marked stateliness* (om. MS, LC, CB)
  422–3   *He . . .* RAINA (om. MS, LC, CB)
    423   *seamy side* Archer focussed on this phrase in his review in the *World* (25 April
         1894).
    437   Shaw originally (MS) placed here the scene between Catherine and Raina that
         now occurs at ll. 700–39 below.

CATHERINE

Oh, Paul, cant you spare Sergius for a few moments? Raina has
hardly seen him yet. Perhaps I can help you to settle about the   440
regiments.

SERGIUS [*protesting*]

My dear madam, impossible: you—

CATHERINE [*stopping him playfully*]

You stay here, my dear Sergius: theres no hurry. I have a word or   445
two to say to Paul. [SERGIUS *instantly bows and steps back*] Now,
dear [*taking* PETKOFF's *arm*]: come and see the electric bell.

PETKOFF

Oh, very well, very well.

They go into the house together affectionately. SERGIUS, *left*   450
alone with RAINA, *looks anxiously at her, fearing that she is still*
offended. She smiles, and stretches out her arms to him.

SERGIUS [*hastening to her*]

Am I forgiven?

RAINA [*placing her hands on his shoulders as she looks up at him*   455
with admiration and worship]

My hero! My king!

SERGIUS

My queen! [*He kisses her on the forehead*]

RAINA   460

How I have envied you, Sergius! You have been out in the
world, on the field of battle, able to prove yourself there worthy
of any woman in the world; whilst I have had to sit at home
inactive – dreaming – useless – doing nothing that could give
me the right to call myself worthy of any man.   465

SERGIUS

Dearest: all my deeds have been yours. You inspired me. I have
gone through the war like a knight in a tournament with his
lady looking down at him!

450–2   (*Exit R into house, followed by* MOTHER. JUANA *rises and comes down with out-
stretched hands.* SERGIUS *advances towards her. They check themselves with a
common impulse and look round to assure themselves that no one is looking. Then
they resume the movement and meet R between the table and the house* MS). Shaw
revised this again in LC, CB/R; Sergius' 'anxiously' was introduced in HL.

457   *king* (darling MS, LC, CB)

459   (s.d. om. MS, LC, CB; *He kisses her on the forehead with holy awe* HL, US)

RAINA 470

And you have never been absent from my thoughts for a moment. [*Very solemnly*] Sergius: I think we two have found the higher love. When I think of you, I feel that I could never do a base deed, or think an ignoble thought.

SERGIUS 475

My lady and my saint! [*He clasps her reverently*]

RAINA [*returning his embrace*]

My lord and my—

SERGIUS

Sh – sh! Let *me* be the worshipper, dear. You little know how 480 unworthy even the best man is of a girl's pure passion!

RAINA

I trust you. I love you. You will never disappoint me, Sergius. [LOUKA *is heard singing within the house. They quickly release each other*] I cant pretend to talk indifferently before her: my 485 heart is too full. [LOUKA *comes from the house with her tray. She goes to the table, and begins to clear it, with her back turned to them*] I will get my hat; and then we can go out until lunch time. Wouldnt you like that?

SERGIUS 490

Be quick. If you are away five minutes, it will seem five hours. [RAINA *runs to the top of the steps, and turns there to exchange looks with him and wave him a kiss with both hands. He looks after her with emotion for a moment; then turns slowly away, his face radiant with the loftiest exaltation. The movement shifts his* 495 *field of vision, into the corner of which there now comes the tail of* LOUKA's *double apron. His attention is arrested at once. He takes a stealthy look at her, and begins to twirl his moustache mischievously, with his left hand akimbo on his hip. Finally, striking the ground with his heels in something of a cavalry swagger, he strolls* 500

473 *the higher love* Shaw directed that Sergius sigh showily at this phrase (*CPB*, p. 75; BL Add Ms 50644).

478 *my –* (my g – [i.e. god] HL, US)

483 Originally Raina began her speech: 'Let us worship together at the shrine of love' (MS).

491 *Be quick* (CB/R adds s.d.: *Go to foot of steps*)

494–501 *his face . . . says* Original s.d. are more concise; Sergius' 'face radiant' is omitted, but his melodramatic moustache twirling is retained (MS, LC, CB). In rehearsal notes, Shaw stressed that Sergius should coordinate touching his moustache with Louka's singing (*CPB*, p. 75).

over to the other side of the table, opposite her, and says] Louka:
do you know what the higher love is?

LOUKA [*astonished*]

No, sir.

SERGIUS   505

Very fatiguing thing to keep up for any length of time, Louka.
One feels the need of some relief after it.

LOUKA [*innocently*]

Perhaps you would like some coffee, sir? [*She stretches her hand
across the table for the coffee pot*]   510

SERGIUS [*taking her hand*]

Thank you, Louka.

LOUKA [*pretending to pull*]

Oh, sir, you know I didnt mean that. I'm surprised at you!

SERGIUS [*coming clear of the table and drawing her with him*]   515

I am surprised at myself, Louka. What would Sergius, the hero
of Slivnitza, say if he saw me now? What would Sergius, the
apostle of the higher love, say if he saw me now? What would
the half dozen Sergiuses who keep popping in and out of this
handsome figure of mine say if they caught us here? [*Letting go*   520
her hand and slipping his arm dexterously round her waist] Do
you consider my figure handsome, Louka?

LOUKA

Let me go, sir. I shall be disgraced. [*She struggles: he holds her
inexorably*] Oh, *will* you let go?   525

SERGIUS [*looking straight into her eyes*]

No.

LOUKA

Then stand back where we cant be seen. Have you no common
sense?   530

SERGIUS

Ah! thats reasonable. [*He takes her into the stableyard gateway,
where they are hidden from the house*]

LOUKA [*plaintively*]

I may have been seen from the windows: Miss Raina is sure to   535
be spying about after you.

515–22   Shaw never revised this speech, indicating his firm conception of a central aspect
of Sergius' character.

SERGIUS [*stung: letting her go*]

Take care, Louka. I may be worthless enough to betray the higher love; but do not you insult it.

LOUKA [*demurely*] 540

Not for the world, sir, I'm sure. May I go on with my work, please, now?

SERGIUS [*again putting his arm round her*]

You are a provoking little witch, Louka. If you were in love with me, would you spy out of windows on me? 545

LOUKA

Well, you see, sir, since you say you are half a dozen different gentlemen all at once, I should have a great deal to look after.

SERGIUS [*charmed*]

Witty as well as pretty. [*He tries to kiss her*] 550

LOUKA [*avoiding him*]

No: I dont want your kisses. Gentlefolk are all alike: you making love to me behind Miss Raina's back; and she doing the same behind yours.

SERGIUS [*recoiling a step*] 555

Louka!

LOUKA

It shews how little you really care.

SERGIUS [*dropping his familiarity, and speaking with freezing politeness*] 560

If our conversation is to continue, Louka, you will please remember that a gentleman does not discuss the conduct of the lady he is engaged to with her maid.

LOUKA

It's so hard to know what a gentleman considers right. I 565 thought from your trying to kiss me that you had given up being so particular.

SERGIUS [*turning from her and striking his forehead as he comes back into the garden from the gateway*]

Devil! devil! 570

538–9 *I may . . . insult it* (Do not wound the higher love MS, LC, CB)
  544 *witch* (devil MS)
551–620 See Appendix I for the initial, deleted version (MS) in which Shaw intended to reintroduce Bluntschli here rather than later in the act.
559–60 *dropping . . . politeness* (*With the utmost dignity* MS, LC, CB)

LOUKA

Ha! ha! I expect one of the six of you is very like me, sir; though
I am only Miss Raina's maid. [She goes back to her work at the
table, taking no further notice of him]

SERGIUS [speaking to himself]   575

Which of the six is the real man? thats the question that torments me. One of them is a hero, another a buffoon, another a
humbug, another perhaps a bit of a blackguard. [He pauses,
and looks furtively at LOUKA as he adds, with deep bitterness]
And one, at least, is a coward: jealous, like all cowards. [He goes   580
to the table] Louka.

LOUKA

Yes?

SERGIUS

Who is my rival?   585

LOUKA

You shall never get that out of me, for love or money.

SERGIUS

Why?

LOUKA   590

Never mind why. Besides, you would tell that I told you; and I
should lose my place.

SERGIUS [holding out his right hand in affirmation]

No! on the honor of a – [He checks himself; and his hand drops,
nerveless, as he concludes sardonically] – of a man capable of   595
behaving as I have been behaving for the last five minutes. Who
is he?

LOUKA

I dont know. I never saw him. I only heard his voice through
the door of her room.   600

SERGIUS

Damnation! How dare you?

LOUKA [retreating]

Oh, I mean no harm: youve no right to take up my words like
that. The mistress knows all about it. And I tell you that if that   605

575–85   (om. MS, which substitutes: SERGIUS (Drawing her back by the wrist) Only a
         maid. Luga: you are a little fiend incarnate. Who is the other fellow?)
   602   Damnation! Shaw thought Sergius should be 'Explosive–frighten her. Almost
         strike her' (CPB, p. 81).
 604–5   youve no . . . like that (She hid him there to save his life. I'd have done the same for
         any man I cared for MS)

51

gentleman ever comes here again, Miss Raina will marry him, whether he likes it or not. I know the difference between the sort of manner you and she put on before one another and the real manner.

    SERGIUS *shivers as if she had stabbed him. Then, setting his*   610
face like iron, he strides grimly to her, and grips her above the elbows with both hands.

SERGIUS

Now listen you to me.

LOUKA [*wincing*]   615

Not so tight: youre hurting me.

SERGIUS

That doesnt matter. You have stained my honor by making me a party to your eavesdropping. And you have betrayed your mistress.   620

LOUKA [*writhing*]

Please—

SERGIUS

That shews that you are an abominable little clod of common clay, with the soul of a servant. [*He lets her go as if she were*   625
an unclean thing, and turns away, dusting his hands of her, to the bench by the wall, where he sits down with averted head, meditating gloomily]

LOUKA [*whimpering angrily with her hands up her sleeves, feeling her bruised arms*]   630

You know how to hurt with your tongue as well as with your hands. But I dont care, now Ive found out that whatever clay I'm made of, youre made of the same. As for her, she's a liar; and her fine airs are a cheat; and I'm worth six of her. [*She shakes the pain off hardily; tosses her head; and sets to work to put*   635
the things on the tray]

    He looks doubtfully at her. She finishes packing the tray, and laps the cloth over the edges, so as to carry all out together. As she stoops to lift it, he rises.

625–8   *He lets her . . . gloomily* (*He lets her go, dusting his hands of her* MS, LC, CB)

52

SERGIUS   640

Louka! [*She stops and looks defiantly at him*] A gentleman
has no right to hurt a woman under any circumstances. [*With
profound humility, uncovering his head*] I beg your pardon.

LOUKA

That sort of apology may satisfy a lady. Of what use is it to a   645
servant?

SERGIUS [*rudely crossed in his chivalry, throws it off with a bitter
laugh, and says slightingly*]

Oh! you wish to be paid for the hurt? [*He puts on his shako, and
takes some money from his pocket*]   650

LOUKA [*her eyes filling with tears in spite of herself*]

No: I want my hurt made well.

SERGIUS [*sobered by her tone*]

How?

She rolls up her left sleeve; clasps her arm with the thumb and   655
fingers of her right hand; and looks down at the bruise. Then she
raises her head and looks straight at him. Finally, with a superb
gesture, she presents her arm to be kissed. Amazed, he looks at her;
at the arm; at her again; hesitates; and then, with shuddering
intensity, exclaims Never! *and gets away as far as possible from her.* 660

Her arm drops. Without a word, and with unaffected dignity,
she takes her tray, and is approaching the house when RAINA
returns, wearing a hat and jacket in the height of the Vienna
fashion of the previous year, 1885. LOUKA *makes way proudly for*
her, and then goes into the house.   665

RAINA

I'm ready. Whats the matter? [*Gaily*] Have you been flirting
with Louka?

SERGIUS [*hastily*]

No, no. How can you think such a thing?   770

RAINA [*ashamed of herself*]

Forgive me, dear: it was only a jest. I am so happy today.

---

649   *shako* a tall, round, peaked military hat with a plume or feather
660   *Never!* (No, I'll be damned if I will MS; Never! Never! LC, CB)
663–4 *Vienna fashion* Together with London, Paris, and Berlin, Vienna was a centre for
       high fashion.
667   *Whats the matter?* (MS adds: 'SERGIUS (*Half to himself*) I am ashamed – ashamed
       in my very soul', a line deleted in LC, CB)

He goes quickly to her, and kisses her hand remorsefully. CATHERINE
comes out and calls to them from the top of the steps.

CATHERINE [*coming down to them*]   675

I am sorry to disturb you, children; but Paul is distracted over
those three regiments. He doesnt know how to send them to
Philippopolis; and he objects to every suggestion of mine. You
must go and help him, Sergius. He is in the library.

RAINA [*disappointed*]   680

But we are just going out for a walk.

SERGIUS

I shall not be long. Wait for me just five minutes. [*He runs up
the steps to the door*]

RAINA [*following him to the foot of the steps and looking up at him*   685
with timid coquetry]

I shall go round and wait in full view of the library windows. Be
sure you draw father's attention to me. If you are a moment
longer than five minutes, I shall go in and fetch you, regiments
or no regiments.   690

SERGIUS [*laughing*]

Very well. [*He goes in*]

RAINA *watches him until he is out of her sight. Then, with a
perceptible relaxation of manner, she begins to pace up and down
the garden in a brown study.*   695

CATHERINE

Imagine their meeting that Swiss and hearing the whole story!
The very first thing your father asked for was the old coat we
sent him off in. A nice mess you have got us into!

RAINA [*gazing thoughtfully at the gravel as she walks*]   700
The little beast!

CATHERINE

Little beast! What little beast?

688–90   *If you . . . regiments* (om. MS)
  695   *brown study* musing gloomily
  700   *gazing . . . walks* (*Reflecting* MS, LC, CB)
700–39   Shaw originally (MS) placed this scene following line 437 above. ' "The little
         beast" should come at the end of a sort of reverie or blue study during which you
         pay not the least attention to the mother's scolding' (Shaw's advice to Alma
         Murray in 1894, *CL*, I, p. 423).

RAINA

To go and tell! Oh, if I had him here, I'd cram him with   705
chocolate creams til he couldnt ever speak again!

CATHERINE

Dont talk such stuff. Tell me the truth, Raina. How long was he
in your room before you came to me?

RAINA [*whisking round and recommencing her march in the*   710
opposite direction]
Oh, I forget.

CATHERINE

You cannot forget! Did he really climb up after the soldiers were
gone; or was he there when that officer searched the room?   715

RAINA

No. Yes: I think he must have been there then.

CATHERINE

You *think!* Oh, Raina! Raina! Will anything ever make you
straightforward? If Sergius finds out, it will be all over between   720
you.

RAINA [*with cool impertinence*]
Oh, I know Sergius is your pet. I sometimes wish you could
marry him instead of me. You would just suit him. You would
pet him, and spoil him, and mother him to perfection.   725

CATHERINE [*opening her eyes very widely indeed*]
Well, upon my word!

RAINA [*capriciously: half to herself*]
I always feel a longing to do or say something dreadful to
him – to shock his propriety – to scandalize the five senses out   730
of him. [*To* CATHERINE, *perversely*] I dont care whether he
finds out about the chocolate cream soldier or not. I half hope
he may. [*She again turns and strolls flippantly away up the path*
to the corner of the house]

---

721 Here Shaw deleted two original speeches (MS):
   JUANA
      I wonder is Sergius as great a fool as he thinks he is.
   MOTHER
      A fool! Sergius a fool!
   This idea is thus postponed until III, 619. 'Fool' and its variants occur twelve
   times in the play, forming another leitmotif that plays against 'professional'.
723 'Oh, I know Sergius is YOUR pet! Keep slow, and perverse, and mischievous – slow
   – *molto trascinando* [dragging]' (Halstan).

CATHERINE   735

And what should I be able to say to your father, pray?

RAINA [*over her shoulder, from the top of the two steps*]

Oh, poor father! As if *he* could help himself! [*She turns the corner and passes out of sight*]

CATHERINE [*looking after her, her fingers itching*]   740

Oh, if you were only ten years younger! [LOUKA *comes from the house with a salver, which she carries hanging down by her side*] Well?

LOUKA

Theres a gentleman just called, madam. A Serbian officer.   745

CATHERINE [*flaming*]

A Serb! And how dare he – [*checking herself bitterly*] Oh, I forgot. We are at peace now. I suppose we shall have them calling every day to pay their compliments. Well: if he is an officer why dont you tell your master? He is in the library with   750 Major Saranoff. Why do you come to me?

LOUKA

But he asks for you, madam. And I dont think he knows who you are: he said the lady of the house. He gave me this little ticket for you. [*She takes a card out of her bosom; puts it on the*   755 *salver; and offers it to* CATHERINE]

CATHERINE [*reading*]

'Captain Bluntschli'? Thats a German name.

LOUKA

Swiss, madam, I think.   760

CATHERINE [*with a bound that makes* LOUKA *jump back*]

Swiss! What is he like?

LOUKA [*timidly*]

He has a big carpet bag, madam.

CATHERINE   765

Oh Heavens! he's come to return the coat. Send him away: say we're not at home: ask him to leave his address and I'll write to him. Oh stop: that will never do. Wait! [*She throws herself into a chair to think it out.* LOUKA *waits*] The master and Major Saranoff are busy in the library, arnt they?   770

746–51 Catherine was originally less aggressive: 'MOTHER (*Interrupting*) Tell the general. He is in the library with Colonel Sergius. Why do you come to me?' (MS, LC, CB).
766 *coat* (clothes MS)
767–8 *write to* (communicate with MS)

LOUKA

Yes, madam.

CATHERINE [*decisively*]

Bring the gentleman out here at once. [*Peremptorily*] And be
very polite to him. Dont delay. Here [*impatiently snatching the*   775
salver from her]: leave that here; and go straight back to him.

LOUKA

Yes, madam [*going*]

CATHERINE

Louka!   780

LOUKA [*stopping*]

Yes, madam.

CATHERINE

Is the library door shut?

LOUKA   785

I think so, madam.

CATHERINE

If not, shut it as you pass through.

LOUKA

Yes, madam [*going*]   790

CATHERINE

Stop! [LOUKA *stops*] He will have to go that way [*indicating the*
gate of the stableyard] Tell Nicola to bring his bag here after
him. Dont forget.

LOUKA [*surprised*]   795

His bag?

CATHERINE

Yes: here: as soon as possible. [*Vehemently*] Be quick! [LOUKA
runs into the house. CATHERINE *snatches her apron off and*
throws it behind a bush. She then takes up the salver and uses it   800
as a mirror, with the result that the handkerchief tied round her
head follows the apron. A touch to her hair and a shake to her

774   *Peremptorily* (*imperatively* US, GR; s.d. om. MS, LC, CB)

792–4   Several deleted s.d. (MS) indicate Shaw's concern about stage management. *Dont*
        forget deleted in CB/R.

798–811   *Yes . . . appeal* (Yes, *here*, as soon as possible. (*Exit* LUGA) Oh how, how can a man
        be such a fool! Such a moment to select! (*She takes up the salver and uses it as a*
        mirror to settle her hair and prepare herself for the visitor. When she hears him
        coming she puts it down. Enter LUGA, *followed by the man of adventure in Juana's*
        room. He looks much smarter than before. The MOTHER *rises and bows. He bows.*
        LUGA *goes out R. Immediately the* MOTHER *approaches him hurriedly*) MS, LC, CB)

57

dressing gown make her presentable] Oh, how? how? *how* can a
man be such a fool! Such a moment to select! [LOUKA *appears
at the door of the house, announcing* Captain Bluntschli. *She*   805
*stands aside at the top of the steps to let him pass before she goes
in again. He is the man of the midnight adventure in* RAINA's
*room, clean, well brushed, smartly uniformed, and out of trouble,
but still unmistakably the same man. The moment* LOUKA's *back
is turned,* CATHERINE *swoops on him with impetuous, urgent,*   810
coaxing appeal] Captain Bluntschli: I am *very* glad to see you;
but you must leave this house at once. [*He raises his eyebrows]*
My husband has just returned with my future son-in-law; and
they know nothing. If they did, the consequences would be
terrible. You are a foreigner: you do not feel our national ani-   815
mosities as we do. We still hate the Serbs: the effect of the peace
on my husband has been to make him feel like a lion baulked of
his prey. If he discovers our secret, he will never forgive me; and
my daughter's life will hardly be safe. Will you, like the chival-
rous gentleman and soldier you are, leave at once before he   820
finds you here?

BLUNTSCHLI [*disappointed, but philosophical]*

At once, gracious lady. I only came to thank you and return the
coat you lent me. If you will allow me to take it out of my bag
and leave it with your servant as I pass out, I need detain you   825
no further. [*He turns to go into the house]*

CATHERINE [*catching him by the sleeve]*

Oh, you must not think of going back that way. [*Coaxing him
across to the stable gates]* This is the shortest way out. Many
thanks. So glad to have been of service to you.   830
Good bye.

BLUNTSCHLI

But my bag?

CATHERINE

It shall be sent on. You will leave me your address.   835

---

807 *midnight* DE (om. MS, etc)
811–21 In Shaw's initial version (MS), Catherine and Bluntschli pretend they have never
met.
816 *as we do* (MS adds and then deletes: 'The peace makes no difference to our feelings')
829 *way out* (... out – along that path and through the wicket in the great wooden
gates (*Pointing L*) MS)

BLUNTSCHLI

True. Allow me. [*He takes out his card-case, and stops to write his address, keeping* CATHERINE *in an agony of impatience. As he hands her the card,* PETKOFF, *hatless, rushes from the house in a fluster of hospitality, followed by* SERGIUS]   840

PETKOFF [*as he hurries down the steps*]

My dear Captain Bluntschli–

CATHERINE

Oh Heavens! [*She sinks on the seat against the wall*]

PETKOFF [*too preoccupied to notice her as he shakes* BLUNTSCHLI'*s   845
hand heartily*]

Those stupid people of mine thought I was out here, instead of in the – haw! – library [*he cannot mention the library without betraying how proud he is of it*] I saw you through the window. I was wondering why you didnt come in. Saranoff is with me: 850
you remember him, dont you?

SERGIUS [*saluting humorously, and then offering his hand with great charm of manner*]

Welcome, our friend the enemy!

PETKOFF   855

No longer the enemy, happily. [*Rather anxiously*] I hope youve called as a friend, and not about horses or prisoners.

CATHERINE

Oh, quite as a friend, Paul. I was just asking Captain Bluntschli to stay to lunch; but he declares he must go at once.   860

SERGIUS [*sardonically*]

Impossible, Bluntschli. We want you here badly. We have to send on three cavalry regiments to Philippopolis; and we dont in the least know how to do it.

BLUNTSCHLI [*suddenly attentive and businesslike*]   865

Philippopolis? The forage is the trouble, I suppose.

---

840 Originally Sergius enters at line 851 (MS, LC, CB)

844 (s.d. om. MS; *Sinks on to seat L.* CB/R)

856–7 *I hope . . . prisoners* (I hope youve come as a friend, and not on business MS, LC, CB, US)

860 Shaw originally placed the substance of ll. 951–966 at this point (MS).

864 *do it* (MS adds: 'You remember your opinion of my soldiership', which is retained accidentally in CB)

866 *Philippopolis* (MS, LC, CB add: 'Oh, that's easy')

PETKOFF [*eagerly*]

Yes: thats it. [*To* SERGIUS] He sees the whole thing at once.

BLUNTSCHLI

I think I can shew you how to manage that. 870

SERGIUS

Invaluable man! Come along! [*Towering over* BLUNTSCHLI, *he puts his hand on his shoulder and takes him to the steps,* PETKOFF *following*]

RAINA *comes from the house as* BLUNTSCHLI *puts his foot on* 875
the first step.

RAINA

Oh! The chocolate cream soldier!

BLUNTSCHLI *stands rigid.* SERGIUS, *amazed, looks at* RAINA, *then at* PETKOFF, *who looks back at him and then at his wife.* 880

CATHERINE [*with commanding presence of mind*]

My dear Raina, dont you see that we have a guest here? Captain Bluntschli: one of our new Serbian friends.

RAINA *bows:* BLUNTSCHLI *bows.*

RAINA 885

How silly of me! [*She comes down into the centre of the group, between* BLUNTSCHLI *and* PETKOFF] I made a beautiful

870 *I think . . . that* (*Confidently*) I can shew you how to settle that easily enough MS, LC, CB)

877 (s.d. *recoiling* MS, LC, CB; *completely losing her presence of mind* HL, US, GR)

878 'The incident of Raina's coming upon Bluntschli . . . and losing her presence of mind so completely as to betray herself by her exclamation "Oh! The chocolate cream soldier" is not intelligible as you play it. I don't object to your treatment, as it belongs to your feeling about the part; but it gives away the situation. Nothing but a bouncing exclamation of surprise, quite sudden and spontaneous, followed by a very evident moment of confusion as you realize what you have done, will make the audience understand what has happened. If the steps had been placed according to my design there would have been no difficulty; you would have burst upon Bluntschli and the audience the instant you stepped through the door, with the light full on you' (Shaw's advice to Alma Murray in 1894, *CL,* I, p. 438).

879–80 (MS, LC, CB preface s.d. with *Sensation,* used frequently in nineteenth-century melodramas)

ornament this morning for the ice pudding; and that stupid
Nicola has just put down a pile of plates on it and spoilt it. [*To*
BLUNTSCHLI, *winningly*] I hope you didnt think that you were   890
the chocolate cream soldier, Captain Bluntschli.

BLUNTSCHLI [*laughing*]

I assure you I did. [*Stealing a whimsical glance at her*] Your
explanation was a relief.

PETKOFF [*suspiciously, to* RAINA]   895

And since when, pray, have you taken to cooking?

CATHERINE

Oh, whilst you were away. It is her latest fancy.

PETKOFF [*testily*]

And has Nicola taken to drinking? He used to be careful enough.   900
First he shews Captain Bluntschli out here when he knew
quite well I was in the library; and then he goes downstairs and
breaks Raina's chocolate soldier. He must – [NICOLA *appears at
the top of the steps with the bag. He descends; places it respect-
fully before* BLUNTSCHLI; *and waits for further orders. General*   905
amazement. NICOLA, *unconscious of the effect he is producing,*
looks perfectly satisfied with himself. When PETKOFF *recovers*
his power of speech, he breaks out at him with] Are you mad,
Nicola?

NICOLA [*taken aback*]   910

Sir?

PETKOFF

What have you brought that for?

NICOLA

My lady's orders, major. Louka told me that–   915

CATHERINE [*interrupting him*]

My orders! Why should I order you to bring Captain Bluntschli's
luggage out here? What are you thinking of, Nicola?

NICOLA [*after a moment's bewilderment, picking up the bag as*
he addresses BLUNTSCHLI *with the very perfection of servile*   920
discretion]

893   *I assure you I did* (Well, for the moment I was puzzled MS, LC, CB)
904   *the bag* DE (*a carpet bag* MS, etc.)
906–8   NICOLA . . . *him with* (s.d. om. MS, LC, CB)
913   *What . . . for?* (What the devil have you brought that for? MS)
919–21   *after a moment . . . discretion* (*Recovering himself with admirable presence of*
         mind after a moment's bewilderment, and picking up the bag as he addresses
         [BLUNTSCHLI] MS, LC, CB)

I beg your pardon, captain, I am sure. [*To* CATHERINE] My
fault, madam: I hope youll overlook it. [*He bows, and is going to
the steps with the bag, when* PETKOFF *addresses him angrily*]

PETKOFF   925

Youd better go and slam that bag, too, down on Miss Raina's ice
pudding! [*This is too much for* NICOLA. *The bag drops from his
hand almost on his master's toes, eliciting a roar of*] Begone, you
butter-fingered donkey.

NICOLA [*snatching up the bag, and escaping into the house*]   930
Yes, major.

CATHERINE

Oh, never mind, Paul: dont be angry.

PETKOFF [*blustering*]

Scoundrel! He's got out of hand while I was away. I'll teach   935
him. Infernal blackguard! The sack next Saturday! I'll clear out
the whole establishment – [*He is stifled by the caresses of his wife
and daughter, who hang round his neck, petting him*]

CATHERINE ⎱ [*together*]   ⎧ Now, now, now, it mustnt be
RAINA   ⎰   ⎨ Wow, wow, wow: not on your   940
                                  ⎩
                        ⎧ angry. He meant no harm. Be good to
                        ⎪ first day at home. I'll make another ice
                        ⎨ please me, dear. Sh-sh-sh-sh!
                        ⎪ pudding. Tch-ch-ch!
                        ⎩

PETKOFF [*yielding*]   945

Oh well, never mind. Come, Bluntschli: lets have no more
nonsense about going away. You know very well youre not going
back to Switzerland yet. Until you do go back youll stay with us.

927–47   *This is too . . . going away* The original version of this scene (MS), which most
         versions follow, is much briefer:
         MICHAELOFF (*Dropping the bag in his amazement*)
             Sir!
         MOTHER
             Oh never mind, Paul, dont be angry.
         PETKOFF
             Begone, you butterfingered donkey.
         MICHAELOFF
             Yes sir (*Exit with bag R*)
         PETKOFF
             Now Bluntschli, let's have no more nonsense about your having to go away.
         The extended version is only in DE.
934–45   *Infernal . . . yielding* (om. HL, US, GR)

RAINA

  Oh, do, Captain Bluntschli. 950

PETKOFF [to CATHERINE]

  Now, Catherine: it's of you he's afraid. Press him; and he'll stay.

CATHERINE

  Of course I shall be only too delighted if [appealingly] Captain

  Bluntschli really wishes to stay. He knows my wishes. 955

BLUNTSCHLI [in his driest military manner]

  I am at madam's orders.

SERGIUS [cordially]

  That settles it!

PETKOFF [heartily] 960

  Of course!

RAINA

  You see you *must* stay.

BLUNTSCHLI [smiling]

  Well, if I must, I must. 965

    Gesture of despair from CATHERINE.

950 (LC, CB add s.d.: 'CATH: *is thunderstruck by* RAINA's *treachery*'; MS varies slightly)

955 *He knows my wishes* placed after *madam's orders* (957) in MS

960–3 Originally (MS) Raina spoke Petkoff's line and vice versa.

966 (MS adds: End of Act I
                Positions
         Ser, Bl, Juana, Petk, Mother
              Nicola)

ACT III

In the library after lunch. It is not much of a library. Its literary
equipment consists of a single fixed shelf stocked with old paper
covered novels, broken backed, coffee stained, torn and thumbed;
and a couple of little hanging shelves with a few gift books on them:
the rest of the wall space being occupied by trophies of war and the   5
chase. But it is a most comfortable sitting room. A row of three large
windows shews a mountain panorama, just now seen in one of its
friendliest aspects in the mellowing afternoon light. In the corner next
the right hand window a square earthenware stove, a perfect tower of
glistening pottery, rises nearly to the ceiling and guarantees plenty of   10
warmth. The ottoman is like that in Raina's room, and similarly
placed; and the window seats are luxurious with decorated cushions.
There is one object, however, hopelessly out of keeping with its
surroundings. This is a small kitchen table, much the worse for wear,
fitted as a writing table with an old canister full of pens, an eggcup   15
filled with ink, and a deplorable scrap of heavily used pink blotting
paper.

At the side of this table, which stands to the left of anyone facing
the window, BLUNTSCHLI is hard at work with a couple of maps
before him, writing orders. At the head of it sits SERGIUS, who is   20
supposed to be also at work, but is actually gnawing the feather of a
pen, and contemplating BLUNTSCHLI's quick, sure, businesslike
progress with a mixture of envious irritation at his own incapacity
and awestruck wonder at an ability which seems to him almost
miraculous, though its prosaic character forbids him to esteem it. The   25
MAJOR is comfortably established on the ottoman, with a newspaper
in his hand and the tube of his hookah within easy reach.
CATHERINE sits at the stove, with her back to them, embroidering.
RAINA, reclining on the divan, is gazing in a daydream out at the
Balkan landscape, with a neglected novel in her lap.   30

Act III Originally designated Act II (MS); it began with a scene between Bluntschli
and Juana. Unlike LC, Alps and Balkans has not been deleted in CB.

1–33   MS provides variant, but similar s.d., which are somewhat briefer in LC, CB.

12   cushions (US, GR add: Little Turkish tables, one of them with an elaborate hookah
on it, and a screen to match them, complete the handsome effect of the furnishing)

27   hookah an oriental tobacco pipe with a long tube that passes through water

The door is on the same side as the stove, farther from the
window. The button of the electric bell is at the opposite side, behind
BLUNTSCHLI.

PETKOFF [*looking up from his paper to watch how they are getting*
    on at the table]   35

Are you sure I cant help you in any way, Bluntschli?
BLUNTSCHLI [*without interrupting his writing or looking up*]

Quite sure, thank you. Saranoff and I will manage it.
SERGIUS [*grimly*]

Yes: we'll manage it. He finds out what to do; draws up the   40
orders; and I sign em. Division of labor! [BLUNTSCHLI *passes*
him a paper] Another one? Thank you. [*He plants the paper*
squarely before him; sets his chair carefully parallel to it; and signs
with his cheek on his elbow and his protruded tongue following
the movements of his pen] This hand is more accustomed to the   45
sword than to the pen.

PETKOFF

It's very good of you, Bluntschli: it is indeed, to let yourself be
put upon in this way. Now are you *quite* sure I can do nothing?
CATHERINE [*in a low warning tone*]   50

You can stop interrupting, Paul.
PETKOFF [*starting and looking round at her*]

Eh? Oh! Quite right, my love: quite right. [*He takes his news-*
paper up again, but presently lets it drop] Ah, you havnt
been campaigning, Catherine: you dont know how pleasant it is   55

---

31   *The door* Shaw believed this was an innovation: 'the real novelty, which nobody
     off the stage noticed, was that Major Petkoff's library had only one door' (*CL*, II,
     p. 686).

41   *Division of labor* A concept in Adam Smith's 1776 book, *An Inquiry into the*
     Nature and Causes of the Wealth of Nations. 'The greatest improvement in the pro-
     ductive powers of labour, and the greater part of the skill, dexterity, and judgment
     with which it is anywhere directed, or applied, seem to have been the effects of the
     division of labour' (book I, chapter 1).

44–5 *his cheek ... his pen* (om. MS; *the air of a man resolutely performing a difficult and*
     dangerous feat US, GR) CB/R adds the business of Bluntschli directing Sergius
     where to sign. 'During rehearsals of the 1911 production, Shaw had Bluntschli
     provoke the explanation [ll. 45–6] by reacting to Sergius' manner of signing his
     name: "When Serg lays his head on his arm to sign, look at him in alarm"'
     (Dukore, *Director*, p. 95).

for us to sit here, after a good lunch, with nothing to do but enjoy ourselves. Theres only one thing I want to make me thoroughly comfortable.

CATHERINE

What is that? 60

PETKOFF

My old coat. I'm not at home in this one: I feel as if I were on parade.

CATHERINE

My dear Paul, how absurd you are about that old coat! It must 65
be hanging in the blue closet where you left it.

PETKOFF

My dear Catherine, I tell you Ive looked there. Am I to believe
my own eyes or not? [CATHERINE *rises and crosses the room to*
press the button of the electric bell] What are you shewing off that 70
bell for? [*She looks at him majestically, and silently resumes her*
chair and her needlework] My dear: if you think the obstinacy
of your sex can make a coat out of two old dressing gowns of
Raina's, your waterproof, and my mackintosh, youre mistaken.
Thats exactly what the blue closet contains at present. 75

NICOLA *presents himself.*

CATHERINE

Nicola: go to the blue closet and bring your master's old coat
here: the braided one he wears in the house.

NICOLA

Yes, madam. [*He goes out*]

PETKOFF 80

Catherine.

CATHERINE

Yes, Paul.

PETKOFF

I bet you any piece of jewellery you like to order from Sofia 85
against a week's housekeeping money that the coat isnt there.

---

57 *ourselves* (MS, LC, CB add: [CATHERINE] *glances at the busy Bluntschli; then*
resumes her embroidery)

77 (US, GR add s.d.: *unmoved by Petkoff's sally*)

CATHERINE

Done, Paul! 90

PETKOFF [*excited by the prospect of a gamble*]

Come: heres an opportunity for some sport. Wholl bet on it?
Bluntschli: I'll give you six to one.

BLUNTSCHLI [*imperturbably*]

It would be robbing you, major. Madam is sure to be right. 95
[*Without looking up, he passes another batch of papers to* SERGIUS]

SERGIUS [*also excited*]

Bravo, Switzerland! Major: I bet my best charger against an
Arab mare for Raina that Nicola finds the coat in the blue
closet. 100

PETKOFF [*eagerly*]

Your best char—

CATHERINE [*hastily interrupting him*]

Dont be foolish, Paul. An Arabian mare will cost you 50,000
levas. 105

RAINA [*suddenly coming out of her picturesque revery*]

Really, mother, if you are going to take the jewellery, I dont see
why you should grudge me my Arab.

NICOLA *comes back with the coat, and brings it to* PETKOFF,
who can hardly believe his eyes. 110

CATHERINE

Where was it, Nicola?

NICOLA

Hanging in the blue closet, madam.

PETKOFF 115

Well, I *am* d—

CATHERINE [*stopping him*]

Paul!

PETKOFF

I could have sworn it wasnt there. Age is beginning to tell 120
on me. I'm getting hallucinations. [*To* NICOLA] Here: help me

---

93 *six to one* (unlimited odds MS, LC, CB, HL)
101–2 (om. MS, LC. Petkoff's line was added in CB/R)
110 *can hardly believe his eyes* (*is thunderstruck* MS, LC, CB)
116 *d* – (damned! MS)

67

to change. Excuse me, Bluntschli. [*He begins changing coats,* NICOLA *acting as valet*] Remember: I didnt take that bet of yours, Sergius. Youd better give Raina that Arab steed yourself, since youve roused her expectations. Eh, Raina? [*He looks round at her; but she is again rapt in the landscape. With a little gush of parental affection and pride, he points her out to them, and says*] She's dreaming, as usual.   125

SERGIUS

Assuredly she shall not be the loser.   130

PETKOFF

So much the better for her. *I* shant come off so cheaply, I expect. [*The change is now complete.* NICOLA *goes out with the discarded coat*] Ah, now I feel at home at last. [*He sits down and takes his newspaper with a grunt of relief*]   135

BLUNTSCHLI [*to* SERGIUS, *handing a paper*]

Thats the last order.

PETKOFF [*jumping up*]

What! Finished?

BLUNTSCHLI   140

Finished.

PETKOFF [*with childlike envy*]

Havnt you anything for *me* to sign?

BLUNTSCHLI

Not necessary. His signature will do.   145

PETKOFF [*inflating his chest and thumping it*]

Ah well, I think weve done a thundering good day's work. Can I do anything more?

BLUNTSCHLI

You had better both see the fellows that are to take these.   150
[SERGIUS *rises*] Pack them off at once; and shew them that Ive marked on the orders the time they should hand them in by. Tell them that if they stop to drink or tell stories – if theyre five minutes late, theyll have the skin taken off their backs.

126–7   *With a . . . and says* (om. MS, LC, CB)

141   *Finished* (Except in DE, Petkoff here moves to Sergius and looks '*curiously over his left shoulder*' as he signs. MS, LC, CB add: 'SERGIUS. My dear Bluntschli: you are the greatest commander of ancient or modern times. With ambition you would be a Napoleon or an Alexander (*Signs*)'

SERGIUS [*stiffening indignantly*]   155

I'll say so. [*He strides to the door*] And if one of them is man enough to spit in my face for insulting him, I'll buy his discharge and give him a pension. [*He goes out*]

BLUNTSCHLI [*confidentially*]

Just see that he talks to them properly, major, will you?   160

PETKOFF [*officiously*]

Quite right, Bluntschli, quite right. I'll see to it. [*He goes to the door importantly, but hesitates on the threshold*] By the bye, Catherine, you may as well come too. They'll be far more frightened of you than of me.   165

CATHERINE [*putting down her embroidery*]

I daresay I had better. You would only splutter at them. [*She goes out*, PETKOFF *holding the door for her and following her*]

BLUNTSCHLI

What an army! They make cannons out of cherry trees; and the   170
officers send for their wives to keep discipline! [*He begins to fold and docket the papers*]

    RAINA, *who has risen from the divan, marches slowly down the room with her hands clasped behind her, and looks mischievously at him.*   175

RAINA

You look ever so much nicer than when we last met. [*He looks up, surprised*] What have you done to yourself?

---

158   *He goes out* (*He strides out, his humanity deeply outraged* US, GR)

167   *splutter at them* (CB/R adds: 'PET: Yes, and you splutter so much better than I do').

170   *army* DE (country MS, etc.)

176   'Now when B. & R. are left alone for the first time since their adventure six months before, the whole atmosphere should change; and this is done quite simply by waiting a little and then *commencing* (not continuing) in a new tone, at a new speed, in this case much slower and obviously provocative and mischievous' (Shaw's advice to Stella Campbell [Raina] in 1919, *Theatrics*, p. 152).

176–375   In 1907 Shaw provided Lillah McCarthy with extensive notes on specific business in this scene, and felt that Raina was a demanding role: 'The transitions are very sudden, and come one after the other with fearful rapidity. But on the other hand, when once they become mechanical, their effect is certain. To get the maximum of effect you must feed Bluntschli very carefully. Your high horse will not amuse the audience unless he knocks you off it; and you must take care to caracole very proudly indeed every time a fall is coming' (see *Theatrics*, pp. 86–7).

BLUNTSCHLI

Washed; brushed; good night's sleep and breakfast. Thats all.   180

RAINA

Did you get back safely that morning?

BLUNTSCHLI

Quite, thanks.

RAINA   185

Were they angry with you for running away from Sergius's charge?

BLUNTSCHLI [*grinning*]

No: they were glad; because theyd all just run away themselves.

RAINA [*going to the table, and leaning over it towards him*]   190

It must have made a lovely story for them: all that about me and my room.

BLUNTSCHLI

Capital story. But I only told it to one of them: a particular friend.   195

RAINA

On whose discretion you could absolutely rely?

BLUNTSCHLI

Absolutely.

RAINA   200

Hm! He told it all to my father and Sergius the day you exchanged the prisoners. [*She turns away and strolls carelessly across to the other side of the room*]

BLUNTSCHLI [*deeply concerned, and half incredulous*]

No! You dont mean that, do you?   205

RAINA [*turning, with sudden earnestness*]

I do indeed. But they dont know that it was in this house you took refuge. If Sergius knew, he would challenge you and kill you in a duel.

BLUNTSCHLI   210

Bless me! then dont tell him.

186–7 'A little more malice is wanted in the "Were they angry with you for running away from Sergius's charge" & so on' (Shaw's advice to Alma Murray in 1894, *CL*, I, p. 423).

188 *grinning* DE (om. MS, etc)

200–59 See Appendix I for Shaw's first version of this scene, which he deleted in MS.

RAINA

Please be serious, Captain Bluntschli. Can you not realize what
it is to me to deceive him? I want to be quite perfect with
Sergius: no meanness, no smallness, no deceit. My relation to   215
him is the one really beautiful and noble part of my life. I hope
you can understand that.

BLUNTSCHLI [*sceptically*]

You mean that you wouldnt like him to find out that the story
about the ice pudding was a – a – a – You know.   220

RAINA [*wincing*]

Ah, dont talk of it in that flippant way. I lied: I know it. But I
did it to save your life. He would have killed you. That was the
second time I ever uttered a falsehood. [BLUNTSCHLI *rises
quickly and looks doubtfully and somewhat severely at her*] Do   225
you remember the first time?

BLUNTSCHLI

I! No. Was I present?

RAINA

Yes; and I told the officer who was searching for you that you   230
were not present.

BLUNTSCHLI

True. I should have remembered it.

RAINA [*greatly encouraged*]

Ah, it is natural that you should forget it first. It cost you noth- 235
ing: it cost me a lie! A lie!

*She sits down on the ottoman, looking straight before her with
her hands clasped round her knee.* BLUNTSCHLI, *quite touched,
goes to the ottoman with a particularly reassuring and considerate
air, and sits down beside her.*   240

212–14   RAINA ... *deceive him?* In an attempt to secure the correct tone, Shaw tried several vari-
         ants, including 'RAINA (*full of reproach for his levity*) Can you realize what it is to me to
         deceive him?' (US, GR). Shaw advised Margaret Halstan: ' "Ah, can you [not] realize &c"
         very musically reproachful – "Didst thou but know" sort of tone' (Halstan). In 1919
         Shaw's advice to Stella Campbell was 'If you like, you may alter "Can you realize what it
         is to me to deceive him" to "Please be serious, Captain Bluntschli. Can you not realize
         what it is to me to deceive him &c&c&c." ' Shaw thought this change, adopted in DE,
         was 'an improvement. But be ready to prompt [Robert] Loraine [Bluntschli] in case the
         alteration dries him up and leaves him speechless' (*CL*, III, p. 645).

   222   *flippant way* (MS, LC, CB add: 'as if it was a trifle'. Shaw might have eliminated the
         line because 'trifle' created a pun with 'pudding')

232–3   (om. MS, LC, CB; i.e. Raina's speech continues uninterrupted)

238–40   *quite ... air* (om. MS, LC, CB)

BLUNTSCHLI

My dear young lady, dont let this worry you. Remember: I'm a
soldier. Now what are the two things that happen to a soldier so
often that he comes to think nothing of them? One is hearing
people tell lies [RAINA *recoils*]: the other is getting his life saved   245
in all sorts of ways by all sorts of people.

RAINA [*rising in indignant protest*]

And so he becomes a creature incapable of faith and of
gratitude.

BLUNTSCHLI [*making a wry face*]   250

Do you like gratitude? I dont. If pity is akin to love, gratitude is
akin to the other thing.

RAINA

Gratitude! [*Turning on him*] If you are incapable of gratitude
you are incapable of any noble sentiment. Even animals are   255
grateful. Oh, I see now exactly what you think of me! You were
not surprised to hear me lie. To you it was something I probably
did every day! every hour!! That is how men think of women.
[*She paces the room tragically*]

BLUNTSCHLI [*dubiously*]   260

Theres reason in everything. You said youd told only two lies
in your whole life. Dear young lady: isnt that rather a short
allowance? I'm quite a straightforward man myself; but it
wouldnt last me a whole morning.

RAINA [*staring haughtily at him*]   265

Do you know, sir, that you are insulting me?

BLUNTSCHLI

I cant help it. When you strike that noble attitude and speak in
that thrilling voice, I admire you; but I find it impossible to
believe a single word you say.   270

RAINA [*superbly*]

Captain Bluntschli!

BLUNTSCHLI [*unmoved*]

Yes?

RAINA [*standing over him, as if she could not believe her senses*]   275

Do you mean what you said just now? Do you *know* what you
said just now?

247   (s.d. om. MS; *Rising* LC, CB)
259   *tragically* (*melodramatically* US)
268   *When you strike that* DE (When you get into that MS, etc.)
275   *standing over him* (om. MS, LC; *coming a little towards him* CB/R, US, GR)

72

BLUNTSCHLI

I do.

RAINA [*gasping*]   280

I! I!!! [*She points to herself incredulously, meaning 'I, Raina Petkoff
tell lies!' He meets her gaze unflinchingly. She suddenly sits down
beside him, and adds, with a complete change of manner from the
heroic to a babyish familiarity*] How did you find me out?

BLUNTSCHLI [*promptly*]   285

Instinct, dear young lady. Instinct, and experience of the world.

RAINA [*wonderingly*]

Do you know, you are the first man I ever met who did not take
me seriously?

BLUNTSCHLI   290

You mean, dont you, that I am the first man that has ever taken
you quite seriously?

RAINA

Yes: I suppose I *do* mean that. [*Cosily, quite at her ease with
him*] How strange it is to be talked to in such a way! You know,   295
Ive always gone on like that.

BLUNTSCHLI

You mean the –?

RAINA

I mean the noble attitude and the thrilling voice. [*They laugh   300
together*] I did it when I was a tiny child to my nurse. *She* believed
in it. I do it before my parents. *They* believe in it. I do it before
Sergius. *He* believes in it.

BLUNTSCHLI

Yes: he's a little in that line himself, isnt he?   305

RAINA [*startled*]

Oh! Do you think so?

BLUNTSCHLI

You know him better than I do.

RAINA   310

I wonder – I *wonder* is he? If I thought *that* –! [*Discouraged*]
Ah, well: what does it matter? I suppose now youve found me
out, you despise me.

280–4   (RAINA (*Incredulously*) I! I!! (*She sits down beside him*) How did you find me out?'
        MS, LC, CB) After 'beside him' Shaw wrote in '*and adds, with a complete change of
        manner from the heroic to the familiar*' (LC, CB)

297–8   DE (om. MS, etc)

300–1   *They laugh together* DE (om. MS, etc)

BLUNTSCHLI [*warmly, rising*]

    No, my dear young lady, no, no, no a thousand times. It's part   315
of your youth: part of your charm. I'm like all the rest of them:
the nurse, your parents, Sergius: I'm your infatuated admirer.

RAINA [*pleased*]

    Really?

BLUNTSCHLI [*slapping his breast smartly with his hand, German*   320
fashion]

    Hand aufs Herz! Really and truly.

RAINA [*very happy*]

    But what did you think of me for giving you my portrait?

BLUNTSCHLI [*astonished*]   325

    Your portrait! You never gave me your portrait.

RAINA [*quickly*]

    Do you mean to say you never got it?

BLUNTSCHLI

    No. [*He sits down beside her, with renewed interest, and says,*   330
with some complacency] When did you send it to me?

RAINA [*indignantly*]

    I did not send it to you. [*She turns her head away, and adds,*
reluctantly] It was in the pocket of that coat.

BLUNTSCHLI [*pursing his lips and rounding his eyes*]   335

    Oh-o-oh! I never found it. It must be there still.

RAINA [*springing up*]

    There still! for my father to find the first time he puts his hand
in his pocket! Oh, how could you be so stupid?

BLUNTSCHLI [*rising also*]   340

    It doesnt matter: I suppose it's only a photograph: how can he
tell who it was intended for? Tell him he put it there himself.

RAINA [*bitterly*]

    Yes: that is so clever! isnt it? [*Distractedly*] Oh! what shall I do?

BLUNTSCHLI   345

    Ah, I see. You wrote something on it. That was rash.

RAINA [*vexed almost to tears*]

    Oh, to have done such a thing for *you*, who care no more –
except to laugh at me – oh! Are you sure nobody has
touched it?   350

---

322 *Hand aufs Herz* Hand on heart (i.e. I am telling the truth)
333 *send it to you* (MS added: 'How dare you? BLUNT – Well, but how –?', which CB/R
    deleted)

BLUNTSCHLI

Well. I cant be quite sure. You see, I couldnt carry it about
with me all the time: one cant take much luggage on active
service.

RAINA   355

What did you do with it?

BLUNTSCHLI

When I got through to Pirot I had to put it in safe keeping
somehow. I thought of the railway cloak room; but thats the
surest place to get looted in modern warfare. So I pawned it.   360

RAINA

Pawned it!!!

BLUNTSCHLI

I know it doesnt sound nice; but it was much the safest plan.
I redeemed it the day before yesterday. Heaven only knows   365
whether the pawnbroker cleared out the pockets or not.

RAINA [*furious: throwing the words right into his face*]

You have a low shopkeeping mind. You think of things that
would never come into a gentleman's head.

BLUNTSCHLI [*phlegmatically*]   370

Thats the Swiss national character, dear lady. [*He returns to the
table*]

RAINA

Oh, I wish I had never met you. [*She flounces away, and sits at
the window fuming*]   375

    LOUKA *comes in with a heap of letters and telegrams on her
salver, and crosses, with her bold free gait, to the table. Her left
sleeve is looped up to the shoulder with a brooch, shewing her
naked arm, with a broad gilt bracelet covering the bruise.*

---

368   *shopkeeping mind* England was often called a nation of shopkeepers, a notion
      traceable to Adam Smith (although frequently ascribed to Napoleon): 'To found
      a great empire for the sole purpose of raising up a people of customers may at
      first sight appear a project fit only for a nation of shopkeepers. It is, however, a
      project altogether unfit for a nation of shopkeepers; but extremely fit for a nation
      whose government is influenced by shopkeepers' (*Wealth of Nations*, book IV,
      chapter 7).

376   *letters and telegrams* A common nineteenth-century theatrical device used to
      resolve plots artificially. Shaw defended his use of the device here in *CL*, II, pp.
      686–7.

LOUKA [*to* BLUNTSCHLI]   380

For you. [*She empties the salver with a fling on to the table*] The
messenger is waiting. [*She is determined not to be civil to an
enemy, even if she must bring him his letters*]

BLUNTSCHLI [*to* RAINA]

Will you excuse me: the last postal delivery that reached me was   385
three weeks ago. These are the subsequent accumulations. Four
telegrams: a week old. [*He opens one*] Oho! Bad news!

RAINA [*rising and advancing a little remorsefully*]

Bad news?

BLUNTSCHLI   390

My father's dead. [*He looks at the telegram with his lips pursed,
musing on the unexpected change in his arrangements.* LOUKA
crosses herself hastily]

RAINA

Oh, how very sad!   395

BLUNTSCHLI

Yes: I shall have to start for home in an hour. He has left a lot of
big hotels behind him to be looked after. [*He takes up a fat
letter in a long blue envelope*] Here's a whacking letter from the
family solicitor. [*He pulls out the enclosures and glances over*   400
them] Great Heavens! Seventy! Two hundred! [*In a crescendo of
dismay*] Four hundred! Four *thousand*!! Nine thousand six
hundred!!! What on earth am I to do with them all?

RAINA [*timidly*]

Nine thousand hotels?   405

BLUNTSCHLI

Hotels! nonsense. If you only knew! Oh, it's too ridiculous!
Excuse me: I must give my fellow orders about starting. [*He
leaves the room hastily, with the documents in his hand*]

---

381   *with a fling* (om. MS, LC, CB; *Recklessly* US, GR)
388   *rising . . . remorsefully* (*Anxiously* MS, LC, CB)
392–3   LOUKA *crosses herself hastily* (om. US, GR)
397–403 Shaw advised Stella Campbell in 1919 to 'play [react] a little to B's "leave for home
        in an hour," which is a dreadful blow. It explains the tragic tone of "What does *he*
        care: what does *any* soldier care?" ' (*Theatrics*, p. 152). 'In an hour' conflicts with
        Bluntschli's later 'In the morning I shall be off home' (682). Shaw wanted
        Bluntschli to 'pile it up more' when reading the letter (*CPB*, p. 123).

LOUKA [*knowing instinctively that she can annoy* RAINA *by*   410
disparaging BLUNTSCHLI]

He has not much heart, that Swiss. He has not a word of grief
for his poor father.

RAINA [*bitterly*]

Grief! A man who has been doing nothing but killing people   415
for years! What does he care? What does any soldier care? [*She
goes to the door, restraining her tears with difficulty*]

LOUKA

Major Saranoff has been fighting too; and he has plenty of
heart left. [RAINA, *at the door, draws herself up haughtily and*   420
goes out] Aha! I thought you wouldnt get much feeling out of
your soldier. [*She is following* RAINA *when* NICOLA *enters with
an armful of logs for the stove*]

NICOLA [*grinning amorously at her*]

Ive been trying all the afternoon to get a minute alone with   425
you, my girl. [*His countenance changes as he notices her arm*]
Why, what fashion is that of wearing your sleeve, child?

LOUKA [*proudly*]

My own fashion.

NICOLA   430

Indeed! If the mistress catches you, she'll talk to you. [*He puts
the logs down, and seats himself comfortably on the ottoman*]

LOUKA

Is that any reason why *you* should take it on yourself to talk
to me?   435

NICOLA

Come! dont be so contrary with me. Ive some good news for
you. [*She sits down beside him. He takes out some paper money.
LOUKA, with an eager gleam in her eyes, tries to snatch it; but he
shifts it quickly to his left hand, out of her reach*] See! a twenty   440
leva bill! Sergius gave me that, out of pure swagger. A fool and

---

410–11   (s.d. added DE; *tauntingly* US, GR)

  412   *Swiss* (gentleman MS, LC, CB; US, GR add: 'though he is so fond of the Servians')

  420   Initially Shaw extended the duologue between Raina and Louka to include
Raina noticing Louka's arrangement of her sleeve; he transferred that business to
Nicola (426–7).

421–2   Shaw's second use of a one-sentence soliloquy.

426–37   *His countenance . . . contrairy with me* (deleted CB/R)

his money are soon parted. Theres ten levas more. The Swiss
gave me that for backing up the mistress's and Raina's lies
about him. *He's* no fool, he isnt. You should have heard old
Catherine downstairs as polite as you please to me, telling me   445
not to mind the Major being a little impatient; for they knew
what a good servant I was – after making a fool and liar of me
before them all! The twenty will go to our savings; and you
shall have the ten to spend if youll only talk to me so as to
remind me I'm a human being. I get tired of being a servant   450
occasionally.

LOUKA

Yes: sell your manhood for 30 levas, and buy me for 10! [*Rising
scornfully*] Keep your money. You were born to be a servant. I
was not. When you set up your shop you will only be every-   455
body's servant instead of somebody's servant. [*She goes moodily
to the table and seats herself regally in* SERGIUS'*s chair*]

NICOLA [*picking up his logs, and going to the stove*]

Ah, wait til you see. We shall have our evenings to ourselves;
and I shall be master in my own house, I promise you. [*He*   460
throws the logs down and kneels at the stove]

LOUKA

You shall never be master in mine.

NICOLA [*turning, still on his knees, and squatting down rather
forlornly on his calves, daunted by her implacable disdain*]   465
You have a great ambition in you, Louka. Remember: if any
luck comes to you, it was I that made a woman of you.

LOUKA

You!

NICOLA [*scrambling up and going at her*]   470

Yes, me. Who was it made you give up wearing a couple of
pounds of false black hair on your head and reddening your lips
and cheeks like any other Bulgarian girl! I did. Who taught you

444–8   *You should have ... before them all* (deleted CB/R) In 1919, Shaw directed
      Dorothy Holmes-Gore (Louka) to 'laugh spitefully at "a fool & a liar" ' (see *CPB*,
      p. 127).
453–4   *Yes ... scornfully* (om. MS, LC, CB)
      30 levas A suggestion of the thirty pieces of silver Judas received for betraying
      Christ (Matthew 26:15). Shaw imagined Raina kissing her father in similar terms;
      see note to III, 914–17.
456–7   s.d. DE (placed at line 463 in MS, etc.)
  465   *daunted by her implacable disdain* (om. MS, LC, CB)
  470   *scrambling .. at her* (om. MS, LC, CB; *with dogged self-assertion* US, GR)

to trim your nails, and keep your hands clean, and be dainty
about yourself, like a fine Russian lady? Me: do you hear that?   475
me! [*She tosses her head defiantly; and he turns away, adding,
more coolly*] Ive often thought that if Raina were out of the way,
and you just a little less of a fool and Sergius just a little more of
one, you might come to be one of my grandest customers,
instead of only being my wife and costing me money.   480

LOUKA

I believe you would rather be my servant than my husband. You
would make more out of me. Oh, I know that soul of yours.

NICOLA [*going closer to her for greater emphasis*]

Never you mind my soul; but just listen to my advice. If you   485
want to be a lady, your present behavior to me wont do at all,
unless when we're alone. It's too sharp and impudent; and
impudence is a sort of familiarity: it shews affection for me.
And dont you try being high and mighty with me, either. Youre
like all country girls: you think it's genteel to treat a servant the   490
way I treat a stableboy. Thats only your ignorance; and dont
you forget it. And dont be so ready to defy everybody. Act as if
you expected to have your own way, not as if you expected to
be ordered about. The way to get on as a lady is the same as the
way to get on as a servant: youve got to know your place: thats   495
the secret of it. And you may depend on me to know my place
if you get promoted. Think over it, my girl. I'll stand by you:
one servant should always stand by another.

LOUKA [*rising impatiently*]

Oh, I must behave in my own way. You take all the courage out   500
of me with your cold-blooded wisdom. Go and put those logs
on the fire: thats the sort of thing *you* understand.

  Before NICOLA *can retort,* SERGIUS *comes in. He checks
himself a moment on seeing* LOUKA; *then goes to the stove.*

---

  480 *money* (ll. 497–8 ('Think . . . another') originally added here, but deleted CB/R)
  485–8 *If you want . . . affection for me* (deleted CB/R)
  489–95 *And dont . . . of it* (Holograph addition to HL; You must be quiet in your ways and
        very polite. Dont be so ready to defy everybody: settle yourself down more: take it
        as a matter of course that people will behave properly to you. If you act as if you
        were born to be put upon instead of born to put upon other people, youll never
        make a lady MS. In LC, CB, TX1, 'settle . . . properly to you' is deleted)
  497–8 *Think over it . . . by another* (Placed here in HL; see note to line 480)
  502 *Before* NICOLA *can retort* (om. MS, LC, CB)

79

SERGIUS [*to* NICOLA]   505

I am not in the way of your work, I hope.

NICOLA [*in a smooth, elderly manner*]

Oh no, sir: thank you kindly. I was only speaking to this foolish
girl about her habit of running up here to the library whenever
she gets a chance, to look at the books. Thats the worst of her   510
education, sir: it gives her habits above her station. [*To* LOUKA]
Make that table tidy, Louka, for the Major. [*He goes out
sedately*]

LOUKA, *without looking at* SERGIUS, *pretends to arrange the
papers on the table. He crosses slowly to her, and studies the*   515
arrangement of her sleeve reflectively.

SERGIUS

Let me see: is there a mark there? [*He turns up the bracelet and
sees the bruise made by his grasp. She stands motionless, not looking at him: fascinated, but on her guard*] Ffff! Does it hurt?   520

LOUKA

Yes.

SERGIUS

Shall I cure it?

LOUKA [*instantly withdrawing herself proudly, but still not looking*   525
at him]

No. You cannot cure it now.

SERGIUS [*masterfully*]

Quite sure? [*He makes a movement as if to take her in his arms*]

LOUKA   530

Dont trifle with me, please. An officer should not trifle with a
servant.

SERGIUS [*indicating the bruise with a merciless stroke of his
forefinger*]

That was no trifle, Louka.   535

LOUKA [*flinching; then looking at him for the first time*]

Are you sorry?

SERGIUS [*with measured emphasis, folding his arms*]

I am *never* sorry.

525–6   *but still not looking at him* (om. MS, LC, CB)
528–9   (SERGIUS. Cruel! MS, LC, CB)
533–4   *indicating . . . forefinger* (*pointing to the arm* MS, LC, CB)
   536   *for the first time* (om. MS, LC, CB)

LOUKA [*wistfully*]   540

I wish I could believe a man could be as unlike a woman as
that. I wonder are you really a brave man?

SERGIUS [*unaffectedly, relaxing his attitude*]

Yes: I am a brave man. My heart jumped like a woman's at the
first shot; but in the charge I found that I was brave. Yes: that at   545
least is real about me.

LOUKA

Did you find in the charge that the men whose fathers are poor
like mine were any less brave than the men who are rich like you.

SERGIUS [*with bitter levity*]   550

Not a bit. They all slashed and cursed and yelled like heroes.
Psha! the courage to rage and kill is cheap. I have an English
bull terrier who has as much of that sort of courage as the
whole Bulgarian nation, and the whole Russian nation at its
back. But he lets my groom thrash him, all the same. Thats   555
your soldier all over! No, Louka: your poor men can cut
throats; but they are afraid of their officers; they put up with
insults and blows; they stand by and see one another punished
like children: aye, and help to do it when they are ordered. And
the officers!!! Well [*with a short harsh laugh*] I am an officer.   560
Oh, [*fervently*] give me the man who will defy to the death any
power on earth or in heaven that sets itself up against his own
will and conscience: he alone is the brave man.

LOUKA

How easy it is to talk! Men never seem to me to grow up: they   565
all have schoolboy's ideas. You dont know what true courage is.

545–6 *Yes: that at least is real about me* (LC, etc)

554–5 *and the whole Russian nation at its back* (and the whole English nation too MS,
LC, CB, which was deleted CB/R) Since the phrase was deleted in rehearsal, this
may have been the phrase Bernard Gould (Sergius) inadvertently added at the
first performance, and at which R. Goulding Bright took offence (see
Introduction, p. xxxv, fn 64, and note to ll. 848–51 below). HL revises to 'Russian
nation'.

555–6 *Thats your soldier all over* (om. MS, LC, CB; added CB/R)

555–60 *your poor men . . . an officer* (Present text established in CB/R)

557–60 *but they . . . officers* (but they are curs at heart. They are afraid of their officers MS,
LC)

559 *children* (schoolboys MS)

559–61 *And the officers!!! . . . give* (And the officers are greater curs still – snobs, lick-
spittles, turfhunters. Give . . . MS, LC)

562–3 *that sets . . . conscience* (that claims any superiority to him MS, LC, CB)

563 *he alone is the brave man* Shaw wanted Sergius to deliver this 'to the gallery –
forget her' (*CPB*, p. 133).

SERGIUS [*ironically*]

Indeed! I am willing to be instructed. [*He sits on the ottoman, sprawling magnificently*]

LOUKA   570

Look at me! how much am I allowed to have my own will? I have to get your room ready for you: to sweep and dust, to fetch and carry. How could that degrade me if it did not degrade you to have it done for you? But [*with subdued passion*] if I were Empress of Russia, above everyone in the world, then!! Ah then,   575 though according to you I could shew no courage at all, you should see, you should see.

SERGIUS

What would you do, most noble Empress?

LOUKA   580

I would marry the man I loved, which no other queen in Europe has the courage to do. If I loved you, though you would be as far beneath me as I am beneath you, I would dare to be the equal of my inferior. Would you dare as much if you loved me? No: if you felt the beginnings of love for me you would not   585 let it grow. You would not dare: you would marry a rich man's daughter because you would be afraid of what other people would say of you.

SERGIUS [*bounding up*]

You lie: it is not so, by all the stars! If I loved you, and I were the   590 Czar himself, I would set you on the throne by my side. You know that I love another woman, a woman as high above you as heaven is above earth. And you are jealous of her.

LOUKA

I have no reason to be. She will never marry you now. The man   595 I told you of has come back. She will marry the Swiss.

SERGIUS [*recoiling*]

The Swiss!

571–3   *Look at . . . and carry* (How easy, how cheap, and how vulgar it would be for me to scorn to acknowledge you as my superior – to defy you to the death, as you call it – to have refused this morning to help in getting your room ready for you – sweeping, dusting, fetching and carrying! MS, LC, CB)

575   *above* (superior to MS, LC, CB)

590–1   *You lie . . . himself* (You lie, you little wretch. If I loved you, and I were Prester John or the Emperor of China MS. LC, CB follow MS but add: 'It is not so, by all the stars') Prester John was a legendary medieval Christian emperor of Asia.

LOUKA

A man worth ten of you. Then you can come to me; and I will 600
refuse you. You are not good enough for me. [*She turns to the door*]

SERGIUS [*springing after her and catching her fiercely in his arms*]
I will kill the Swiss; and afterwards I will do as I please with
you. 605

LOUKA [*in his arms, passive and steadfast*]
The Swiss will kill you, perhaps. He has beaten you in love. He
may beat you in war.

SERGIUS [*tormentedly*]
Do you think I believe that she – *she*! whose worst thoughts are 610
higher than your best ones, is capable of trifling with another
man behind my back?

LOUKA

Do you think *she* would believe the Swiss if he told her now
that I am in your arms? 615

SERGIUS [*releasing her in despair*]
Damnation! Oh, damnation! Mockery! mockery everywhere!
everything I think is mocked by everything I do. [*He strikes
himself frantically on the breast*] Coward! liar! fool! Shall I kill
myself like a man, or live and pretend to laugh at myself? [*She* 620
again turns to go] Louka! [*She stops near the door*] Remember:
you belong to me.

LOUKA [*turning*]
What does that mean? An insult?

SERGIUS [*commandingly*] 625
It means that you love me, and that I have had you here in my
arms, and will perhaps have you there again. Whether that is an
insult I neither know nor care: take it as you please. But [*vehemently*] I *will* not be a coward and a trifler. If I choose to love
you, I dare marry you, in spite of all Bulgaria. If these hands 630
ever touch you again, they shall touch my affianced bride.

LOUKA

We shall see whether you dare keep your word. And take care. I
will not wait long.

606   (s.d. om. MS; *In his arms* CB)
619–20   *Coward . . . at myself?* (Ha! Ha! Well, we shall see, we shall see MS, LC, CB)
623   *turning* (om. MS, LC, CB; *quietly* US, GR)

SERGIUS [*again folding his arms and standing motionless in the*   635
middle of the room]

Yes: we shall see. And you shall wait my pleasure.

    BLUNTSCHLI, *much preoccupied, with his papers still in his
hand, enters, leaving the door open for* LOUKA *to go out. He goes
across to the table, glancing at her as he passes.* SERGIUS, *without*   640
altering his resolute attitude, watches him steadily. LOUKA *goes
out, leaving the door open.*

BLUNTSCHLI [*absently, sitting at the table as before, and putting
down his papers*]

Thats a remarkable looking young woman.   645

SERGIUS [*gravely, without moving*]

Captain Bluntschli.

BLUNTSCHLI

Eh?

SERGIUS   650

You have deceived me. You are my rival. I brook no rivals. At six
o'clock I shall be in the drilling-ground on the Klissoura road,
alone, on horseback, with my sabre. Do you understand?

BLUNTSCHLI [*staring, but sitting quite at his ease*]

Oh, thank you: thats a cavalry man's proposal. I'm in the   655
artillery; and I have the choice of weapons. If I go, I shall take
a machine gun. And there shall be no mistake about the
cartridges this time.

SERGIUS [*flushing, but with deadly coldness*]

Take care, sir. It is not our custom in Bulgaria to allow invita-   660
tions of that kind to be trifled with.

BLUNTSCHLI [*warmly*]

Pooh! dont talk to me about Bulgaria. You dont know what
fighting is. But have it your own way. Bring your sabre along.
I'll meet you.   665

SERGIUS [*fiercely delighted to find his opponent a man of spirit*]

Well said, Switzer. Shall I lend you my best horse?

---

648   (s.d. *Catching the change of tone* MS, LC, CB)

652   *Klissoura* a Bulgarian town 75 miles east of Sofia

655–8   Bluntschli's choice of weapons recalls Sergius' chivalric disillusionment with
modern warfare and its dictates: 'Get your enemy at a disadvantage; and never, on
any account, fight him on equal terms' (II, 348–50).

663–4   *You dont . . . is* The sentence gave Shaw some difficulty; one early attempt was:
'You know as much about fighting as the Venetians do about cab driving' (MS).

BLUNTSCHLI

No: damn your horse! thank you all the same, my dear fellow.
[RAINA *comes in, and hears the next sentence*] I shall fight you   670
on foot. Horseback's too dangerous: I dont want to kill you if I
can help it.

RAINA [*hurrying forward anxiously*]

I have heard what Captain Bluntschli said, Sergius. You are
going to fight. Why? [SERGIUS *turns away in silence, and goes to*   675
the stove, where he stands watching her as she continues, to
BLUNTSCHLI] What about?

BLUNTSCHLI

I dont know: he hasnt told me. Better not interfere, dear young
lady. No harm will be done: Ive often acted as sword instructor.   680
He wont be able to touch me; and I'll not hurt him. It will save
explanations. In the morning I shall be off home; and youll
never see me or hear of me again. You and he will then make it
up and live happily ever after.

RAINA [*turning away deeply hurt, almost with a sob in her voice*]   685
I never said I wanted to see you again.

SERGIUS [*striding forward*]

Ha! That is a confession.

RAINA [*haughtily*]

What do you mean?   690

SERGIUS

You love that man!

RAINA [*scandalized*]

Sergius!

SERGIUS   695

You allow him to make love to you behind my back, just as you

---

675–7 (s.d. om. MS, LC, CB; *Sergius looks at Raina then goes to fire* CB/R)
682 *In the morning* 'When you interrupt the challenge scene, Bluntschli tells you not
to be alarmed – he wont hurt Sergius – he has acted as a sword instructor &c &c.
The phrase that stabs you in the speech is "In the morning I shall be off home &
never see you again." That is what makes you forget all about the duel & shew
your feelings in the next speech – "I never said &c." The point seemed to me to
want marking. By the bye, will you point out that "In the morning should be "In
an hour," as he has already received the telegram' (Shaw's advice to Alma Murray
in 1894, *CL*, I, p. 423; and see note to line 397–403 above).
685 *turning . . . voice* (*Turning away hurt* MS, LC, CB; TX1 added the sob in her voice)
686 *I never . . . again* Shaw advised Margaret Halstan to speak the line with 'wounded
heart and throat full of tears. You will get over it before you come to "You are very
solicitous", but the feeling, though more controlled, is the same' (Halstan).

treat me as your affianced husband behind his. Bluntschli: you
knew our relations; you deceived me. It is for that I call you to
account, not for having received favors *I* never enjoyed.

BLUNTSCHLI [*jumping up indignantly*]   700

Stuff! Rubbish! I have received no favors. Why, the young lady
doesnt even know whether I'm married or not.

RAINA [*forgetting herself*]

Oh! [*Collapsing on the ottoman*] *Are* you?

SERGIUS   705

You see the young lady's concern, Captain Bluntschli. Denial is
useless. You have enjoyed the privilege of being received in her
own room, late at night—

BLUNTSCHLI [*interrupting him pepperily*]

Yes, you blockhead! she received me with a pistol at her head.   710
Your cavalry were at my heels. I'd have blown out her brains if
she'd uttered a cry.

SERGIUS [*taken aback*]

Bluntschli! Raina: is this true?

RAINA [*rising in wrathful majesty*]   715

Oh, how dare you, how dare you?

BLUNTSCHLI

Apologize, man: apologize. [*He resumes his seat at the table*]

SERGIUS [*with the old measured emphasis, folding his arms*]

I *never* apologize!   720

RAINA [*passionately*]

This is the doing of that friend of yours, Captain Bluntschli. It
is he who is spreading this horrible story about me. [*She walks
about excitedly*]

BLUNTSCHLI   725

No: he's dead. Burnt alive.

RAINA [*stopping, shocked*]

Burnt alive!

BLUNTSCHLI

Shot in the hip in a woodyard. Couldnt drag himself out. Your   730
fellows' shells set the timber on fire and burnt him, with half a
dozen other poor devils in the same predicament.

720   See note to II, 313.
726–32   Shaw took this story from General Marbot's *Memoirs* (trans. 1892); see 'Dramatic
         Realist', DE, pp. 502–3.
728   *Burnt alive!* Originally said by both Raina and Sergius (MS)
730   *woodyard* (field of standing corn MS, LC, CB; woodyard CB/R)
731   *timber* (corn MS, LC, CB; timber CB/R)

RAINA

How horrible!

SERGIUS   735

And how ridiculous! Oh, war! war! the dream of patriots and
heroes! A fraud, Bluntschli. A hollow sham, like love.

RAINA [*outraged*]

Like love! You say that before me!

BLUNTSCHLI   740

Come, Saranoff: that matter is explained.

SERGIUS

A hollow sham, I say. Would you have come back here if nothing had passed between you except at the muzzle of your pistol?
Raina is mistaken about your friend who was burnt. He was   745
not my informant.

RAINA

Who then? [*Suddenly guessing the truth*] Ah, Louka! my maid!
my servant! You were with her this morning all that time after –
after – Oh, what sort of god is this I have been worshipping!   750
[*He meets her gaze with sardonic enjoyment of her disenchant-
ment. Angered all the more, she goes closer to him, and says, in a
lower, intenser tone*] Do you know that I looked out of the
window as I went upstairs, to have another sight of my hero;
and I saw something I did not understand then. I know now   755
that you were making love to her.

SERGIUS [*with grim humor*]

You saw that?

RAINA

Only too well. [*She turns away, and throws herself on the divan*   760
under the centre window, quite overcome]

SERGIUS [*cynically*]

Raina: our romance is shattered. Life's a farce.

BLUNTSCHLI [*to RAINA, whimsically*]

You see: *he's* found himself out now.   765

745–6   *Raina ... informant* (Our friend who was shot in the corn was not my only
informant MS, LC, CB; Our friend who was burnt was not my only informant
CB/R)

748–9   'How *dare* you? HOW dare you? Intense and splendid dignity – towering – regal.
Who then? (Shock) Ah! ⌒ Louka! My *maid*!! My SERVANT!!! *Dont* hurry. Raina
never hurries' (Halstan). Shaw's use of a fermata between 'ah!' and 'Louka!'
indicates a pause.

SERGIUS [*going to him*]

Bluntschli: I have allowed you to call me a blockhead. You may
now call me a coward as well. I refuse to fight you. Do you
know why?

BLUNTSCHLI   770

No; but it doesnt matter. I didnt ask the reason when you cried
on; and I dont ask the reason now that you cry off. I'm a professional soldier: I fight when I have to, and am very glad to get
out of it when I havnt to. Youre only an amateur: you think
fighting's an amusement.   775

SERGIUS [*sitting down at the table, nose to nose with him*]

You shall hear the reason all the same, my professional. The
reason is that it takes two men – real men – men of heart,
blood and honor – to make a genuine combat. I could no more
fight with you than I could make love to an ugly woman. Youve   780
no magnetism: youre not a man: youre a machine.

BLUNTSCHLI [*apologetically*]

Quite true, quite true. I always *was* that sort of chap. I'm very
sorry.

SERGIUS   785

Psha!

BLUNTSCHLI

But now that youve found that life *isnt* a farce, but something
quite sensible and serious, what further obstacle is there to your
happiness?   790

RAINA [*rising*]

You are very solicitous about my happiness and his. Do you
forget his new love – Louka? It is not you that he must fight
now, but his rival, Nicola.

SERGIUS   795

Rival!! [*Bounding half across the room*]

RAINA

Dont you know that theyre engaged?

SERGIUS

Nicola! Are fresh abysses opening? Nicola!!   800

RAINA [*sarcastically*]

A shocking sacrifice, isnt it? Such beauty! such intellect! such
modesty! wasted on a middle-aged servant man. Really, Sergius,

776   s.d. DE (s.d. om. MS, etc)
783   *I always was that sort of chap* (I always *was* deficient in that way MS, LC, CB)
796   s.d. DE (*Striking his forehead* MS, etc.)

88

you cannot stand by and allow such a thing. It would be unwor-
thy of your chivalry.   805
SERGIUS [*losing all self-control*]
    Viper! Viper! [*He rushes to and fro, raging*]
BLUNTSCHLI
    Look here, Saranoff: youre getting the worst of this.
RAINA [*getting angrier*]   810
    Do you realize what he has done, Captain Bluntschli? He has set
    this girl as a spy on us; and her reward is that he makes love to her.
SERGIUS
    False! Monstrous!
RAINA   815
    Monstrous! [*Confronting him*] Do you deny that she told you
    about Captain Bluntschli being in my room?
SERGIUS
    No; but–
RAINA [*interrupting*]   820
    Do you deny that you were making love to her when she told
    you?
SERGIUS
    No; but I tell you–
RAINA [*cutting him short contemptuously*]   825
    It is unnecessary to tell us anything more. That is quite enough
    for us. [*She turns away from him and sweeps majestically back to
    the window*]
BLUNTSCHLI [*quietly, as* SERGIUS, *in an agony of mortification,
    sinks on the ottoman, clutching his averted head between his fists*] 830
    I told you you were getting the worst of it, Saranoff.
SERGIUS
    Tiger cat!
RAINA [*running excitedly to* BLUNTSCHLI]
    You hear this man calling me names, Captain Bluntschli?   835
BLUNTSCHLI
    What else can he do, dear lady? He must defend himself somehow.
    Come [*very persuasively*]: dont quarrel. What good does it do?

814 *False! Monstrous!* The deleted original, 'Oh, this is monstrous, monstrous' (MS),
     might have evoked Othello's declaration (*Othello*, III.iii.427)
833 Sergius' speech was originally (MS) much longer, and included: 'I *did* make love
     to her, but at the time thought you an angel of light!'. Bluntschli also calls Raina
     an 'angel' (I, 434), possibly evoking associations with *The Angel in the Attic* (see
     Introduction, p. xxi, fn 34)
834–42 (s.d. om. MS)

RAINA, *with a gasp, sits down on the ottoman, and after a vain effort to look vexedly at* BLUNTSCHLI, *falls a victim to her sense of humor, and actually leans back babyishly against the writhing shoulder of* SERGIUS. 840

SERGIUS

Engaged to Nicola! Ha! ha! Ah well, Bluntschli, you are right to take this huge imposture of a world coolly. 845

RAINA [*quaintly to* BLUNTSCHLI, *with an intuitive guess at his state of mind*]

I daresay you think us a couple of grown-up babies, dont you?

SERGIUS [*grinning savagely*]

He does: he does. Swiss civilization nursetending Bulgarian barbarism, eh? 850

BLUNTSCHLI [*blushing*]

Not at all, I assure you. I'm only very glad to get you two quieted. There! there! let's be pleasant and talk it over in a friendly way. Where is this other young lady? 855

RAINA

Listening at the door, probably.

SERGIUS [*shivering as if a bullet had struck him, and speaking with quiet but deep indignation*]

I will prove that that, at least, is a calumny. [*He goes with dignity* 860 *to the door and opens it. A yell of fury bursts from him as he looks out. He darts into the passage, and returns dragging in* LOUKA, *whom he flings violently against the table, exclaiming*] Judge her, Bluntschli. *You*, the cool impartial man: judge the eavesdropper.

LOUKA *stands her ground, proud and silent.* 865

841–2   *actually . . .* SERGIUS (om. MS, LC, CB; *is attacked with a disposition to laugh* US; *can hardly help laughing* GR)

848–51   *grown-up babies* (idiots MS, LC, CB) Shaw's revision (made in HL) reinforces 'nursetending' in *Swiss civilization nursetending Bulgarian barbarism, eh?* (also added HL). Since the 'Swiss civilization' sentence was added after the first production, it cannot be the phrase R. Goulding Bright objected to, as E.J. West suggests tentatively in *Advice to a Young Critic and Other Letters*, 1955, pp. 6–7 (see also note to III, 554–5, and Introduction, p. xxxv).

849   (s.d. om. MS, LC, CB; *grinning a little* US)

858–9   *shivering . . . indignation* (*Exploding again* MS, LC, CB)

864   *the cool impartial man* DE (the moderate, cautious man MS, etc.)

BLUNTSCHLI [*shaking his head*]

    I mustnt judge her. I once listened myself outside a tent when there was a mutiny brewing. It's all a question of the degree of provocation. My life was at stake.

LOUKA   870

    My love was at stake. I am not ashamed.

RAINA [*contemptuously*]

    Your love! Your curiosity, you mean.

LOUKA [*facing her and retorting her contempt with interest*]

    My love, stronger than anything *you* can feel, even for your   875 chocolate cream soldier.

SERGIUS [*with quick suspicion, to* LOUKA]

    What does that mean?

LOUKA [*fiercely*]

    It means–   880

SERGIUS [*interrupting her slightingly*]

    Oh, I remember: the ice pudding. A paltry taunt, girl!

        MAJOR PETKOFF *enters, in his shirtsleeves.*

PETKOFF

    Excuse my shirtsleeves, gentlemen. Raina: somebody has been   885 wearing that coat of mine: I'll swear it. Somebody with a differently shaped back. It's all burst open at the sleeve. Your mother is mending it. I wish she'd make haste: I shall catch cold. [*He looks more attentively at them*] Is anything the matter?

RAINA   890

    No. [*She sits down at the stove, with a tranquil air*]

SERGIUS

    Oh no. [*He sits down at the end of the table, as at first*]

BLUNTSCHLI [*who is already seated*]

    Nothing. Nothing.   895

PETKOFF [*sitting down on the ottoman in his old place*]

    Thats all right. [*He notices* LOUKA] Anything the matter, Louka?

LOUKA

    No, sir.

PETKOFF [*genially*]   900

    Thats all right. [*He sneezes*] Go and ask your mistress for my coat, like a good girl, will you?

---

    871   *stake* (US, GR add s.d.: *Sergius flinches, ashamed of her in spite of himself*)

  879–81 (om. MS, LC, CB, i.e. Sergius' speech continues uninterrupted)

  886–7 *a differently shaped back* DE (bigger shoulders than mine MS, etc.)

NICOLA *enters with the coat.* LOUKA *makes a pretence of having business in the room by taking the little table with the hookah away to the wall near the windows.* 905

RAINA [*rising quickly as she sees the coat on* NICOLA'*s arm*]

Here it is, papa. Give it to me, Nicola; and do you put some more wood on the fire. [*She takes the coat, and brings it to the* MAJOR, *who stands up to put it on.* NICOLA *attends to the fire*]

PETKOFF [*to* RAINA, *teasing her affectionately*] 910

Aha! Going to be very good to poor old papa just for one day after his return from the wars, eh?

RAINA [*with solemn reproach*]

Ah, how can you say that to me, father?

PETKOFF 915

Well, well, only a joke, little one. Come: give me a kiss. [*She kisses him*] Now give me the coat.

RAINA

No: I am going to put it on for you. Turn your back. [*He turns his back and feels behind him with his arms for the sleeves. She* 920 *dexterously takes the photograph from the pocket and throws it on the table before* BLUNTSCHLI, *who covers it with a sheet of paper under the very nose of* SERGIUS, *who looks on amazed, with his suspicions roused in the highest degree. She then helps* PETKOFF *on with his coat*] There, dear! Now are you comfortable? 925

PETKOFF

Quite, little love. Thanks. [*He sits down; and* RAINA *returns to her seat near the stove*] Oh, by the bye, Ive found something funny. Whats the meaning of this? [*He puts his hand into the picked pocket*] Eh? Hallo! [*He tries the other pocket*] Well, I could 930 have sworn –! [*Much puzzled, he tries the breast pocket*]

903–5   NICOLA ... *windows* ([LOUKA] *looks irresolutely at* SERGIUS *and then goes slowly towards the door. Enter* NICOLA *with the coat* MS, LC, CB. CB/R revises this to include the business with the table)

914–17   'In the pocket-picking scene, the line "Ah, how can you say that to me, father?" ought to be in the most pathetic edition of the noble attitude & thrilling voice, leading up to the Judas kiss' (Shaw's advice to Alma Murray in 1894, *CL*, I, p. 423). The whole pick-pocketing scene is redolent of similar scenes in farce and pantomime.

923–4   *with his ... degree* (*utterly mystified and scandalized* MS, LC, CB)

927   *little* (om. MS, LC, CB)

I wonder – [*trying the original pocket*] Where can it –? [*He rises, exclaiming*] Your mother's taken it!

RAINA [*very red*]

Taken what? 935

PETKOFF

Your photograph, with the inscription: 'Raina, to her Chocolate Cream Soldier: a Souvenir.' Now you know theres something more in this than meets the eye; and I'm going to find it out. [*Shouting*] Nicola! 940

NICOLA [*coming to him*]

Sir!

PETKOFF

Did you spoil any pastry of Miss Raina's this morning?

NICOLA 945

You heard Miss Raina say that I did, sir.

PETKOFF

I know that, you idiot. Was it true?

NICOLA

I am sure Miss Raina is incapable of saying anything that is not 950
true, sir.

PETKOFF

Are you? Then I'm not. [*Turning to the others*] Come: do you think I dont see it all? [*He goes to* SERGIUS, *and slaps him on the shoulder*] Sergius: youre the chocolate cream soldier, arnt 955
you?

SERGIUS [*starting up*]

I! A chocolate cream soldier! Certainly not.

932–3 *He rises, exclaiming* (*a light flashes on him* MS, LC, CB; *A light flashes on him; he rises, exclaiming* US, GR)

934 (s.d. om. MS, LC, CB, TX1)

935 *Taken what?* (MS, LC, CB add:
  GENERAL
      Taken something out of my pocket. I knew there was some double dealing going on. Do you know what I found in that pocket?
  JUANA
      I cant imagine, I'm sure.
  These lines were deleted CB/R)

937 *Your photograph* (CB/R adds: 'out of my pocket – your photograph')

941 *coming to him* (*Dropping a log. Comes forward to centre* MS, LC, CB; *dropping a log, and turning* US, GR)

PETKOFF

Not! [*He looks at them. They are all very serious and very con-* 960
scious] Do you mean to tell me that Raina sends things like that
to other men?

SERGIUS [*enigmatically*]

The world is not such an innocent place as we used to think,
Petkoff. 965

BLUNTSCHLI [*rising*]

It's all right, Major. I'm the chocolate cream soldier. [PETKOFF
and SERGIUS *are equally astonished*] The gracious young lady
saved my life by giving me chocolate creams when I was starving: shall I ever forget their flavor! My late friend Stolz told you 970
the story at Pirot. I was the fugitive.

PETKOFF

You! [*He gasps*] Sergius: do you remember how those two
women went on this morning when we mentioned it? [SERGIUS
smiles cynically. PETKOFF *confronts* RAINA *severely*] Youre a nice 975
young woman, arnt you?

RAINA [*bitterly*]

Major Saranoff has changed his mind. And when I wrote that
on the photograph, I did not know that Captain Bluntschli was
married. 980

BLUNTSCHLI [*startled into vehement protest*]

I'm *not* married.

RAINA [*with deep reproach*]

You said you were.

BLUNTSCHLI 985

I did not. I positively did not. I never was married in my life.

PETKOFF [*exasperated*]

Raina: will you kindly inform me, if I am not asking too much,
which of these gentlemen you are engaged to?

961   *things like that* DE (photographic souvenirs MS, etc.)
974–6 SERGIUS . . . *arnt you*? (om MS. which substitutes:
       SERGIUS
          That is nothing to what I have seen since. The universe is a sham.
       GENERAL (*To* RAINA)
          Do you consider it right to send a photographic souvenir to one gentleman
          when you're engaged to another?)
978–9 *when I . . . photograph* (om. MS)
  981 *startled . . . protest* (*Energetically* MS, LC, CB; *much startled – protesting vehemently*
       US)

RAINA   990

To neither of them. *This* young lady [*introducing* LOUKA, *who faces them all proudly*] is the object of Major Saranoff's affections at present.

PETKOFF

Louka! Are you mad, Sergius? Why, this girl's engaged to Nicola.   995

NICOLA

I beg your pardon, sir. There is a mistake. Louka is not engaged to me.

PETKOFF

Not engaged to you, you scoundrel! Why, you had twenty-five   1000
levas from me on the day of your betrothal; and she had that gilt bracelet from Miss Raina.

NICOLA [*with cool unction*]

We gave it out so, sir. But it was only to give Louka protection. She had a soul above her station; and I have been no more than   1005
her confidential servant. I intend, as you know, sir, to set up a shop later on in Sofia; and I look forward to her custom and recommendation should she marry into the nobility. [*He goes out with impressive discretion, leaving them all staring after him*]

PETKOFF [*breaking the silence*]   1010

Well, I *am* – hm!

SERGIUS

This is either the finest heroism or the most crawling baseness. Which is it, Bluntschli?

BLUNTSCHLI   1015

Never mind whether it's heroism or baseness. Nicola's the ablest man Ive met in Bulgaria. I'll make him manager of a hotel if he can speak French and German.

LOUKA [*suddenly breaking out at* SERGIUS]

I have been insulted by everyone here. *You* set them the   1020
example. You owe me an apology.

    SERGIUS, *like a repeating clock of which the spring has been touched, immediately begins to fold his arms.*

---

   996   (s.d *Recovering himself with an obvious effort* MS; *coming forward* US, GR)
1008–9   (s.d. *Exit solemnly* MS, LC, CB)
   1010   (s.d. om. MS; *Looking after him* LC, CB).
   1011   *hm!* (damned MS)
   1013   *This* (That man's conduct CB/R)
1022–3   *like a . . . immediately* (om. MS, LC, CB)

BLUNTSCHLI [*before he can speak*]

It's no use. He never apologizes.   1025

LOUKA

Not to you, his equal and his enemy. To me, his poor servant,
he will not refuse to apologize.

SERGIUS [*approvingly*]

You are right. [*He bends his knee in his grandest manner*]   1030
Forgive me.

LOUKA

I forgive you. [*She timidly gives him her hand, which he kisses*]
That touch makes me your affianced wife.

SERGIUS [*springing up*]   1035

Ah! I forgot that.

LOUKA [*coldly*]

You can withdraw if you like.

SERGIUS

Withdraw! Never! You belong to me. [*He puts his arm about her*]   1040
    CATHERINE *comes in and finds* LOUKA *in* SERGIUS'S *arms,*
    with all the rest gazing at them in bewildered astonishment.

CATHERINE

What does this mean?

        SERGIUS *releases* LOUKA.   1045

PETKOFF

Well, my dear, it appears that Sergius is going to marry Louka
instead of Raina. [*She is about to break out indignantly at him:*
he stops her by exclaiming testily] Dont blame me: Ive nothing
to do with it. [*He retreats to the stove*]   1050

CATHERINE

Marry Louka! Sergius: you are bound by your word to us!

SERGIUS [*folding his arms*]

Nothing binds me.

1025 *He never apologizes* See note to II, 313, and line 1040 below.
1030 *in his grandest manner* (om. MS, LC, CB)
1040 *her* DE (MS, etc. add: *and draws her to him*)
1045 (s.d. om. MS)

BLUNTSCHLI [*much pleased by this piece of common sense*]   1055
    Saranoff: your hand. My congratulations. These heroics of
    yours have their practical side after all. [*To* LOUKA] Gracious
    young lady: the best wishes of a good Republican! [*He kisses her
    hand, to* RAINA's *great disgust, and returns to his seat*]

CATHERINE   1060
    Louka: you have been telling stories.

LOUKA
    I have done Raina no harm.

CATHERINE [*haughtily*]
    Raina!   1065
      RAINA, *equally indignant, almost snorts at the liberty.*

LOUKA
    I have a right to call her Raina: she calls me Louka. I told Major
    Saranoff she would never marry him if the Swiss gentleman
    came back.   1070

BLUNTSCHLI [*rising, much surprised*]
    Hallo!

LOUKA [*turning to* RAINA]
    I thought you were fonder of him than of Sergius. You know
    best whether I was right.   1075

BLUNTSCHLI
    What nonsense! I assure you, my dear Major, my dear Madam,
    the gracious young lady simply saved my life, nothing else. She
    never cared two straws for me. Why, bless my heart and soul,
    look at the young lady and look at me. She, rich, young, beauti-   1080
    ful, with her imagination full of fairy princes and noble natures
    and cavalry charges and goodness knows what! And I, a

1059   *to* RAINA's . . . *seat* (s.d. om. MS, LC, CB)

1066   (RAINA *is equally indignant at the liberty* US, GR)

1068–9   *I have . . . Saranoff* (I am her equal now. I only told Sergius that . . . MS; CB/R
    added: 'I have a right to call her Raina: she calls me Louka') Shaw changed
    'Sergius' to 'Major Saranoff' (HL) in order to postpone Louka's use of the familiar
    until line 1074 where it is associated with 'fonder'.

1074   *Sergius* 'Play [react] to Louka calling Major Saranoff "Sergius" for the first time'
    (Halstan).

1079   *for me* (CB/R adds: '*Louka sits on settee at back RC & smokes cigarette*', a visual
    reminder of her initial unconventional behaviour at the beginning of Act II)

commonplace Swiss soldier who hardly knows what a decent
life is after fifteen years of barracks and battles: a vagabond, a
man who has spoiled all his chances in life through an incur-   1085
ably romantic disposition, a man–

SERGIUS [*starting as if a needle had pricked him and interrupting*
BLUNTSCHLI *in incredulous amazement*]

Excuse me, Bluntschli: *what* did you say had spoiled your
chances in life?   1090

BLUNTSCHLI [*promptly*]

An incurably romantic disposition. I ran away from home
twice when I was a boy. I went into the army instead of into my
father's business. I climbed the balcony of this house when a
man of sense would have dived into the nearest cellar. I came   1095
sneaking back here to have another look at the young lady
when any other man of my age would have sent the coat back–

PETKOFF

My coat!

BLUNTSCHLI   1100

– yes: thats the coat I mean – would have sent it back and gone
quietly home. Do you suppose I am the sort of fellow a young
girl falls in love with? Why, look at our ages! I'm thirty-four: I
dont suppose the young lady is much over seventeen. [*This estimate produces a marked sensation, all the rest turning and staring*   1105
at one another. He proceeds innocently] All that adventure which
was life or death to me, was only a schoolgirl's game to her –
chocolate creams and hide and seek. Heres the proof! [*He takes
the photograph from the table*] Now, I ask you, would a woman
who took the affair seriously have sent me this and written on   1110
it 'Raina, to her Chocolate Cream Soldier: a Souvenir'? [*He
exhibits the photograph triumphantly, as if it settled the matter
beyond all possibility of refutation*]

1086   'Play [react] to "romantic disposition" ' (Halstan). On other occasions, Shaw
       directed that all the characters react to the phrase (*CPB*, p. 161).
1087–8   *starting . . . amazement* (*Interrupting firmly* MS, LC, CB)
   1105   *sensation* For the second time Shaw uses this s.d. common in nineteenth-century
          drama. However, Shaw has inverted the usual situation found in, for example,
          Gilbert and Sullivan's *The Pirates of Penzance*: 'FREDERIC: A lad of twenty-one
          usually looks for a wife of seventeen' (Act I). Bluntschli thinks Raina is seventeen
          and thus too young for a thirty-four year old.
   1109   *table* (MS, LC, CB add: *and exhibiting it*)

PETKOFF

    Thats what I was looking for. How the deuce did it get there?   1115
    [*He comes from the stove to look at it, and sits down at the
    ottoman*]

BLUNTSCHLI [*to* RAINA, *complacently*]

    I have put everything right, I hope, gracious young lady.

RAINA [*going to the table to face him*]   1120

    I quite agree with your account of yourself. You are a romantic
    idiot. [BLUNTSCHLI *is unspeakably taken aback*] Next time,
    I hope you will know the difference between a schoolgirl of
    seventeen and a woman of twenty-three.

BLUNTSCHLI [*stupefied*]   1125

    Twenty-three!

       RAINA *snaps the photograph contemptuously from his hand;
    tears it up; throws the pieces in his face; and sweeps back to her
    former place.*

SERGIUS [*with grim enjoyment of his rival's discomfiture*]   1130

    Bluntschli: my one last belief is gone. Your sagacity is a fraud,
    like everything else. You have less sense than even I!

BLUNTSCHLI [*overwhelmed*]

    Twenty-three! Twenty-three!! [*He considers*] Hm! [*Swiftly making
    up his mind and coming to his host*] In that case, Major Petkoff, I   1135
    beg to propose formally to become a suitor for your daughter's
    hand, in place of Major Saranoff retired.

RAINA

    You dare!

BLUNTSCHLI   1140

    If you were twenty-three when you said those things to me this
    afternoon, I shall take them seriously.

CATHERINE [*loftily polite*]

    I doubt, sir, whether you quite realize either my daughter's
    position or that of Major Sergius Saranoff, whose place you   1145

1116–17 s.d. DE (om. MS, etc)

    1118 *complacently* (TX1 adds *as he bends towards her with his right knee and hand on
    the ottoman*; this was then deleted in HL)

    1120 s.d. DE (*In uncontrollable vexation* MS, etc.)

    1121 ' "I quite agree with your account of yourself" very cold and steady – enormous
    superiority to the creature' (Halstan).

1128–9 *in his face* DE (*at his feet* MS, etc.) *And sweeps . . . place* DE (om. MS, etc)

propose to take. The Petkoffs and the Saranoffs are known as
the richest and most important families in the country. Our
position is almost historical: we can go back for twenty years.

PETKOFF

Oh never mind that, Catherine. [*To* BLUNTSCHLI] We should   1150
be most happy, Bluntschli, if it were only a question of your
position; but hang it, you know, Raina is accustomed to a very
comfortable establishment. Sergius keeps twenty horses.

BLUNTSCHLI

But who wants twenty horses? We're not going to keep a circus.   1155

CATHERINE [*severely*]

My daughter, sir, is accustomed to a first-rate stable.

RAINA

Hush, mother: youre making me ridiculous.

BLUNTSCHLI   1160

Oh well, if it comes to a question of an establishment, here goes!
[*He darts impetuously to the table; seizes the papers in the blue
envelope; and turns to* SERGIUS] How many horses did you say?

SERGIUS

Twenty, noble Switzer.   1165

BLUNTSCHLI

I have two hundred horses. [*They are amazed*] How many
carriages?

SERGIUS

Three.   1170

BLUNTSCHLI

I have seventy. Twenty-four of them will hold twelve inside,
besides two on the box, without counting the driver and
conductor. How many tablecloths have you?

SERGIUS   1175

How the deuce do I know?

1148   Shaw toyed with and rejected the idea of Catherine asking Bluntschli, 'From
       whom, pray, are you descended', and his reply: 'From William Tell. There is a place
       in London where I can get it fixed for a few pounds consideration. My dear
       Madam, for all I know I may be descended from William Tell' (MS). William Tell
       was a legendary Swiss hero.
1155   DE (But what on earth is the use of twenty horses? Why, it's a circus MS etc.)
1157   Presumably the double meaning is intentional.
1160–1223   Auction scenes of various kinds, or the discussion of a man's prospects, are
       common in drama (see, for e.g., *The Taming of the Shrew* (Act II.i), *King Lear* (Act
       I.i), Wilde's *The Importance of Being Earnest* (Act I), Shaw's *Candida* (Act III), and
       Major Barbara (Act I).

BLUNTSCHLI

Have you four thousand?

SERGIUS

No.　1180

BLUNTSCHLI

I have. I have nine thousand six hundred pairs of sheets and
blankets, with two thousand four hundred eider-down quilts. I
have ten thousand knives and forks, and the same quantity of
dessert spoons. I have three hundred servants. I have six palatial　1185
establishments, besides two livery stables, a tea gardens, and a
private house. I have four medals for distinguished services; I
have the rank of an officer and the standing of a gentleman;
and I have three native languages. Shew me any man in
Bulgaria that can offer as much!　1190

PETKOFF [*with childish awe*]

Are you Emperor of Switzerland?

BLUNTSCHLI

My rank is the highest known in Switzerland: I am a free
citizen.　1195

CATHERINE

Then, Captain Bluntschli, since you are my daughter's choice—

RAINA [*mutinously*]

He's not.

CATHERINE [*ignoring her*]　1200

— I shall not stand in the way of her happiness. [PETKOFF *is
about to speak*] That is Major Petkoff's feeling also.

PETKOFF

Oh, I shall be only too glad. Two hundred horses! Whew!

SERGIUS　1205

What says the lady?

RAINA [*pretending to sulk*]

The lady says that he can keep his tablecloths and his
omnibuses. I am not here to be sold to the highest bidder. [*She
turns her back on him*]　1210

1185　*three hundred* DE (six hundred MS, etc.)
1189　*three native languages* Four languages are recognized in Switzerland: German,
　　　French, Italian, and Rumantsch.
1192　(Are you joking, or are you Emperor of Switzerland? MS, LC) *Emperor of
　　　Switzerland* Shaw considered this for the play's title.
1198–9　DE (om. MS, etc.)
1209–10　s.d. DE (om. MS, etc.)

BLUNTSCHLI

I wont take that answer. I appealed to you as a fugitive, a
beggar, and a starving man. You accepted me. You gave me your
hand to kiss, your bed to sleep in, and your roof to shelter me.

RAINA   1215

I did not give them to the Emperor of Switzerland.

BLUNTSCHLI

Thats just what I say. [*He catches her by the shoulders and turns her
face-to-face with him*] Now tell us whom you did give them to.

RAINA [*succumbing with a shy smile*]   1220

To my chocolate cream soldier.

BLUNTSCHLI [*with a boyish laugh of delight*]

Thatll do. Thank you. [*He looks at his watch and suddenly
becomes businesslike*] Time's up, Major. Youve managed those
regiments so well that youre sure to be asked to get rid of some   1225
of the infantry of the Timok division. Send them home by way
of Lom Palanka. Saranoff: dont get married until I come back:
I shall be here punctually at five in the evening on Tuesday
fortnight. Gracious ladies [*His heels click*] good evening [*He
makes them a military bow, and goes*]   1230

SERGIUS

What a man! Is he a man!

1212–14 *I appealed . . . shelter me* Possibly an echo of a biblical variation of the fugitive
theme: 'For I was an hungred, and ye gave me meat: I was thirsty, and ye gave me
drink: I was a stranger, and ye took me in' (Matthew 25:35). *your bed to sleep in*
(HL, etc)

1217–19 (BLUNTSCHLI. To whom then? MS, LC, CB)

1218–19 *He catches . . . with him* (*He catches her hand quickly and looks her straight in the
face as he adds, with confident mastery* US, GR)

1220 (s.d. *Softening* MS, LC, CB)

1226 *Timok* The Timok river flows through eastern Serbia and western Bulgaria

1227 *Lom Palanka* a town in north-west Bulgaria

1229 *Gracious ladies* [*his heels click*] *good evening*. DE (s.d. om. MS, etc.)

1229–30 *He makes . . . goes* (*Bows and goes* MS, LC, CB)

1232 There are several variations on the play's final line. 'Farewell, Switzer.
(BL[UNTSCHLI] *disappears*) What a man! What a man!' (MS, LC, CB). 'What a
man! What a man!' (US, GR; GR emphasizes the second 'what!'). Various other
editions print 'What a man! Is he a man?' (see also Paul Sawyer, 'The last line of
Arms and the Man', SHAW: The Annual of Bernard Shaw Studies, 6 [1986], 123–5).
CB/R deletes Sergius' final speech (ll. 1231–2), and, if accurate, indicates that the
first production in 1894 ended with Bluntschli's exit.

APPENDIX I

Variant scenes

Act II, 164 (additional deleted scene, MS, Notebook A, ff. 51–5)

MOTHER

Is Sergius coming?

FATHER

He will lunch with us. How is Juana?

MOTHER 5

Oh, Juana is always well when she chooses.

FATHER

She has not been anxious or fretting about Sergius, I hope, during the fighting.

MOTHER 10

Not at all. She is too young to feel things really. She was anxious about you at first, but when that passed off she thought of nothing but Sergius's feats in the field. She never seemed to take the man into account, think of the risk he was incurring. Do what you can Paul to hurry on their marriage. Juana is not 15 a bit in earnest about it.

FATHER

Is that a reason for hurrying it on?

MOTHER

Of course. Suppose he finds her out, or she finds herself out 20 and the whole thing is broken off!

FATHER

What do you mean by finding herself out?

MOTHER

You ought to understand that better than I, Paul. She takes after 25 you, not after me.

FATHER

Really, my dear—

MOTHER

Oh yes, really my dear. Take your coffee while it is hot [*Pours it* 30 *out for him*] – Juana has no more real feeling than that coffee pot. She will romance with Sergius, and dress for him like a heroine, and talk like a heroine; *but*–!

FATHER
  But?   35

MOTHER
  Yes. *But*. Mark my words. BUT.

FATHER
  But what?

MOTHER   40
  No, Paul. I will say no more. Juana has made Sergius believe in
  her, hasnt she?

FATHER
  Yes.

MOTHER   45
  Well, she would make anybody else believe in her just the same.
  I say again, do what you can to hurry on their marriage. [*Bell
  again, L*] There he is.

FATHER
  He has lost no time. I thought I should have had an hours start   50
  of him. You must talk to him, my dear, until Juana takes him off
  our hands. He bores my life out about our not promoting him.
  [*Enter* MICHAELOFF (NICOLA)] Michaeloff.

MICH
  Sir?   55

FATHER
  If that is Colonel Sergius, bring him round this way.

MICH
  Yes, sir. [*Exit L*]

MOTHER   60
  He is quite right to complain. He has been treated scandalously
  after his splendid service. Besides, if he is to marry Juana, you
  must get him promoted. He should have been made a lieu-
  tenant general long ago. The country should insist on having at
  least one native general.   65

Act II, 551–620 (original version, MS, Notebook B, ff. 9r, 10r,
11r, 12)

LUGA [LOUKA]
  And then if there was another character. Oh, Miss Juana will
  have enough to do looking after you – between you and the
  Swiss gentleman if it really is you.

SERGIUS   70
   The Switzer has not come courting, Luga: hes a stranger.
LUGA
   Not so strange as you think, perhaps.
SERGIUS
   Why, have you ever seen him before?   75
LUGA
   No; but I have heard his voice before.
SERGIUS
   Where?
LUGA [*slipping away from him*]   80
   I wouldnt tell you that, sir! You shall never get that out of me,
   sir, for love or money.
SERGIUS
   I shall get it out of you by simply waiting for you [to] tell me.
   [*Recapturing her*] Youre dying to tell me, arent you?   85
LUGA
   I dont want to lose my place. You can find out for yourself
   whether he is a stranger or not.
SERGIUS
   How?   90
LUGA
   Go into the hall & open his carpet bag; and you will find
   an old uniform of the general's in it. How did he come to have
   that in his bag if he is not [*sic*] a stranger – see what youll find
   there.   95
SERGIUS [*letting her go, revolted*]
   My dear Luga, a gentleman does not open bags that do not
   belong to him.
LUGA [*archly*]
   Oh, youre not so particular as Miss Juana thinks you, eh sir?   100
SERGIUS [*flinging away from her*]
   Devil, devil, devil.
LUGA
   Ha! ha! I expect one of the six of you is very like me, sir, though
   I'm only a servant.   105
SERGIUS
   Only a servant! Luga, you are a little fiend incarnate. What's in
   the bag?
LUGA
   You wont let on that I told you?   110

SERGIUS

No, on the honor of a – of a man who is capable of behaving as
I have been for the last five minutes.

LUGA

Well, its an old undress uniform of the master's.   115

SERGIUS

Is that all? What of that?

LUGA [*rather contemptuously*]

Would he have a coat of the general's if he were a stranger? Ask
Miss Juana, why she lent it to him.   120

SERGIUS

Lent it to him! Do you mean to say that she knows him as well
as you?

LUGA

Better, sir. I only heard his voice through the door: she was in   125
the room with him.

SERGIUS

It was she who helped him to escape. Listen, you she cat.
[*Seizing her*] He climbed in at the window.

LUGA [*not frightened*]   130
Yes.

SERGIUS [*with grim politeness,* LUGA *holding him by the arms*]
Luga–

LUGA

Not so tight, sir, please – youre hurting me.   135

SERGIUS

That doesnt matter. Let me tell you the whole story. The Swiss
gentleman flying for his life was rescued, nobly rescued, by
your mistress. I heard the whole story from a brother officer of
his. It is a story which shews that your mistress is a noble-   140
hearted lady. You have betrayed her.

LUGA [*writhing*]

Please, sir–

Act III, 200–59 (original version, MS, Notebook B, ff. 17–19, 31)

JUANA

Hm! He told it to my father & Colonel Sergius the day you left   145
him behind after exchanging the prisoners. [*She turns away &
strolls carelessly across L*]

BLUNTSCHLI [*moved*]
>No.

JUANA [*stopping & speaking over her shoulder*]   150
>Yes! If Sergius finds out that it was at our house that you hid, he will challenge you and kill you in a duel.

BLUNTSCHLI
>Then dont tell him. [*She shrugs her shoulders & goes on to her mother's chair, in which she sits. He resumes his work*]   155

JUANA
>Have you ever thought of me since?

BLUNTSCHLI
>No! Too busy. Besides, you are engaged to Don Quixote.

JUANA   160
>How very well you must have been brought up when you even think in such a proper way! [*He puts his chair back; & looks at her with good humor*]

BLUNTSCHLI
>Do you talk to Don Quixote in this disrespectful manner?   165

JUANA
>No. [*Rising suddenly*] And, mind, you must be perfectly respectful in his presence. You must copy his manner, and be chivalrous & dignified & not familiar.

BLUNTSCHLI   170
>Then why dont you keep me at a distance?

JUANA
>How am I, after telling a great thumping lie before you about the ice pudding? If Sergius found me out in such a thing, he would fall down in a fit. Were you surprised?   175

BLUNTSCHLI
>No – not particularly.

[Initially Shaw continued the scene with:

JUANA
>Wretch.   180
>   [*Enter* SERGIUS, *with the* GENERAL *& the* MOTHER *R*]

BLUNTSCHLI
>Sh!

JUANA [*in her grand manner*]
>I am sure you will be as good a friend as you have been a   185
>gallant enemy Captain Bluntschli.

[Shaw deleted the above section, and continued the scene]:

JUANA

Not surprised at my telling a lie! 190

BLUNTSCHLI

I beg your pardon, I forgot that. But it is so very hard for a military man to feel surprised at anyone telling a lie.

JUANA

I never lied but twice in my life; and both times it was to save 195 your life.

BLUNTSCHLI

What! Have you saved my life again?

JUANA

What would your life be worth now if Sergius knew? 200

BLUNTSCHLI

Ah, true: you said he would kill me. I am doubly indebted.

JUANA [*rising in her grand manner*]

And you do not think me untruthful. [*He is at a loss*] Answer me, sir.

APPENDIX II

Additional textual notes

The printed editions of *Arms and the Man* contain many additional stage directions that do not appear in MS, LC, and CB (essentially the text as Shaw first conceived it). While these omitted stage directions are too numerous to include in the footnotes to the play, they are listed here by relevant line number for those readers interested in such matters, and to illustrate how much Shaw fleshed out his original conception after the first production.

Act I, lines 139, 151–2, 156, 160, 163–4, 194, 229–31, 233, 236, 238, 377, 407, 409–11, 424, 430–1, 446, 479–80, 498, 509, 512, 549, 585, 596, 601, 624, 700, 707, 709, 799.

Act II, lines 45, 73, 411–12, 426–8, 642–3, 647–8, 651, 653, 685–6, 693–5, 710–11, 726, 895, 899.

Act III, lines 37, 91, 103, 250, 259, 294–5, 335, 347, 391–3, 410–11, 424, 438–40, 589, 609, 625, 654, 673, 687, 689, 693, 700, 703–4, 709, 715, 723–4, 738, 757, 760–2, 801, 806–7, 825, 827–30, 846–7, 852, 874, 877, 900–1, 910, 913, 954–5, 960–1, 967–8, 983, 1003, 1024, 1041–2, 1048–9, 1055, 1064, 1066, 1071, 1091, 1111–13, 1130, 1134–5, 1156, 1167, 1201–2, 1207, 1222–4.

APPENDIX III

Excerpts from the Preface to *Plays Pleasant* (1898)

Readers of the discourse with which the preceding volume[1] commences will remember that I turned my hand to play-writing when a great deal of talk about 'the New Drama,' followed by the actual establishment of a 'New Theatre' (the Independent),[2] threatened to end in the humiliating discovery that the New Drama, in England at least, was a figment of the revolutionary imagination. This was not to be endured. I had rashly taken up the case; and rather than let it collapse I manufactured the evidence.

Man is a creature of habit. You cannot write three plays and then stop. Besides, the New movement did not stop. In 1894, Florence Farr, who had already produced Ibsen's Rosmersholm, was placed in command of the Avenue Theatre in London for a season on the new lines by Miss A. E. F. Horniman, who had family reasons for not yet appearing openly as a pioneer-manageress. There were, as available New Dramatists, myself discovered by the Independent Theatre (at my own suggestion); Dr John Todhunter, who had been discovered before (his play The Black Cat had been one of the Independent's successes); and Mr W. B. Yeats, a genuine discovery. Dr Todhunter supplied A Comedy of Sighs: Mr Yeats, The Land of Heart's Desire. I, having nothing but unpleasant plays in my desk, hastily completed a first attempt at a pleasant one, and called it Arms and The Man, taking the title from the first line of Dryden's Virgil. It passed for a success, the applause on the first night being as promising as could be wished; and it ran from the 21st of April to the 7th of July. To witness it the public paid £1777 : 5:6, an average of £23 : 2:5 per representation (including nine matinées). A publisher receiving £1700 for a book would have made a satisfactory profit: experts in West End theatrical management will contemplate that figure with a grim smile.[3]

I will not pretend that the modern actor-manager's talent as player can in the nature of things be often associated with exceptional critical insight.

---

1 *Plays Unpleasant.*
2 The Independent Theatre was founded in London in 1891 by J.T Grein with the objective of staging plays on their artistic rather than their commercial merits.
3 On the composition of *Arms and the Man*, and financial aspects of the first production, see Introduction, pp. xvi–xix, xxxv–xxxvi.

As a rule, by the time a manager has experience enough to make him as safe a judge of plays as a Bond Street dealer[4] is of pictures he begins to be thrown out in his calculations by the slow but constant change of public taste, and by his own growing conservatism. But his need for new plays is so great, and the few accredited authors are so little able to keep pace with their commissions, that he is always apt to overrate rather than to under-rate his discoveries in the way of new pieces by new authors. An original work by a man of genius like Ibsen may, of course, baffle him as it baffles many professed critics; but in the beaten path of drama no unacted works of merit, suitable to his purposes, have been discovered; whereas the production, at great expense, of very faulty plays written by novices (not 'backers') is by no means an unknown event. Indeed, to anyone who can estimate, even vaguely, the complicated trouble, the risk of heavy loss, and the initial expense and thought, involved by the production of a play, the ease with which dramatic authors, known and unknown, get their works performed must needs seem a wonder.

Only, authors must not expect managers to invest many thousands of pounds in plays, however fine (or the reverse), which will clearly not attract perfectly commonplace people. Playwriting and theatrical management, on the present commercial basis, are businesses like other businesses, depending on the patronage of great numbers of very ordinary customers. When the managers and authors study the wants of these customers, they succeed: when they do not, they fail. A public-spirited manager, or an author with a keen artistic conscience, may choose to pursue his business with the minimum of profit and the maximum of social usefulness by keeping as close as he can to the highest marketable limit of quality, and constantly feeling for an extension of that limit through the advance of popular culture. An unscrupulous manager or author may aim simply at the maximum of profit with the minimum of risk. These are the opposite poles of our system, represented in practice by our first rate managements at the one end, and the syndicates which exploit pornographic farces at the other. Between them there is plenty of room for most talents to breathe freely: at all events there is a career, no harder of access than any cognate career, for all qualified playwrights who bring the manager what his customers want and understand, or even enough of it to induce them to swallow at the same time a great deal that they neither want nor understand; for the public is touchingly humble in such matters.

4   Bond Street in London's Mayfair district is noted for art dealers' and other elegant shops.

For all that, the commercial limits are too narrow for our social welfare. The theatre is growing in importance as a social organ. Bad theatres are as mischievous as bad schools or bad churches; for modern civilization is rapidly multiplying the class to which the theatre is both school and church. Public and private life become daily more theatrical: the modern Kaiser, Dictator, President or Prime Minister is nothing if not an effective actor; all newspapers are now edited histrionically; and the records of our law courts shew that the stage is affecting personal conduct to an unprecedented extent, and affecting it by no means for the worse, except in so far as the theatrical education of the persons concerned has been romantic: that is, spurious, cheap, and vulgar. The truth is that dramatic invention is the first effort of man to become intellectually conscious. No frontier can be marked between drama and history or religion, or between acting and conduct, nor any distinction made between them that is not also the distinction between the masterpieces of the great dramatic poets and the commonplaces of our theatrical seasons. When this chapter of science is convincingly written, the national importance of the theatre will be as unquestioned as that of the army, the fleet, the Church, the law, and the schools.

For my part, I have no doubt that the commercial limits should be overstepped, and that the highest prestige, with a financial position of reasonable security and comfort, should be attainable in theatrical management by keeping the public in constant touch with the highest achievements of dramatic art. Our managers will not dissent to this: the best of them are so willing to get as near that position as they can without ruining themselves, that they can all point to honorable losses incurred through aiming 'over the heads of the public,' and will no doubt risk such loss again, for the sake of their reputation as artists, as soon as a few popular successes enable them to afford it. But even if it were possible for them to educate the nation at their own private cost, why should they be expected to do it? There are much stronger objections to the pauperization of the public by private doles than were ever entertained, even by the Poor Law Commissioners of 1834, to the pauperization of private individuals by public doles.[5] If we want a theatre which shall be to the drama what the National Gallery and British Museum are to painting and literature, we can get it by endowing it in the same way. In the meantime there are many

---

5   The Poor Law Act of 1834 revised methods of dealing with the indigent, largely forcing
    them into workhouses where conditions were deliberately harsh.

possibilities of local activity. Groups of amateurs can form permanent societies and persevere until they develop into professional companies in established repertory theatres. In big cities it should be feasible to form influential committees, preferably without any actors, critics, or play-wrights on them, and with as many persons of title as possible, for the purpose of approaching one of the leading local managers with a proposal that they shall, under a guarantee against loss, undertake a certain number of afternoon performances of the class required by the committee, in addi-tion to their ordinary business. If the committee is influential enough, the offer will be accepted. In that case, the first performance will be the begin-ning of a classic repertory for the manager and his company which every subsequent performance will extend. The formation of the repertory will go hand in hand with the discovery and habituation of a regular audience for it; and it will eventually become profitable for the manager to multiply the number of performances at his own risk. It might even become worth his while to take a second theatre and establish the repertory permanently in it. In the event of any of his classic productions proving a fashionable success, he could transfer it to his fashionable house and make the most of it there. Such managership would carry a knighthood with it; and such a theatre would be the needed nucleus for municipal or national endow-ment. I make the suggestion quite disinterestedly; for as I am not an academic person, I should not be welcomed as an unacted classic by such a committee; and cases like mine would still leave forlorn hopes like The Independent Theatre its reason for existing. The committee plan, I may remind its critics, has been in operation in London for two hundred years in support of Italian opera.

Returning now to the actual state of things, it is clear that I have no grievance against our theatres. Knowing quite well what I was doing, I have heaped difficulties in the way of the performance of my plays by ignoring the majority of the manager's customers: nay, by positively making war on them. To the actor I have been more considerate, using all my cunning to enable him to make the most of his technical methods; but I have not hesitated on occasion to tax his intelligence very severely, making the stage effect depend not only on *nuances* of execution quite beyond the average skill produced by the routine of the English stage in its present condition, but on a perfectly sincere and straightforward con-ception of states of mind which still seem cynically perverse to most people, and on a goodhumoredly contemptuous or profoundly pitiful attitude towards ethical conventions which seem to them validly heroic or venerable. It is inevitable that actors should suffer more than most of us from the sophistication of their consciousness by romance; and my view of romance as the great heresy to be swept off from art and life – as the food of modern pessimism and the bane of modern self-respect, is far more puzzling to the performers than it is to the pit. It is hard for an actor whose point of honor it is to be a perfect gentleman, to sympathize with an author who regards gentility as a dishonest folly, and gallantry and chivalry as treasonable to women and stultifying to men.

The misunderstanding is complicated by the fact that actors, in their demonstrations of emotion, have made a second nature of stage custom, which is often very much out of date as a representation of contemporary life. Sometimes the stage custom is not only obsolete, but fundamentally wrong: for instance, in the simple case of laughter and tears, in which it deals too liberally, it is certainly not based on the fact, easily enough discoverable in real life, that we only cry now in the effort to bear happiness, whilst we laugh and exult in destruction, confusion, and ruin. When a comedy is performed, it is nothing to me that the spectators laugh: any fool can make an audience laugh. I want to see how many of them, laughing or grave, are in the melting mood. And this result cannot be achieved, even by actors who thoroughly understand my purpose, except through an artistic beauty of execution unattainable without long and arduous practice, and an intellectual effort which my plays probably do not seem serious enough to call forth.

Beyond the difficulties thus raised by the nature and quality of my work, I have none to complain of. I have come upon no ill will, no inaccessibility, on the part of the very few managers with whom I have discussed it. As a rule I find that the actor-manager is over-sanguine, because he has the artist's habit of underrating the force of circumstances and exaggerating the power of the talented individual to prevail against them; whilst I have acquired the politician's habit of regarding the individual, however talented, as having no choice but to make the most of his circumstances. I half suspect that those managers who have had most to do with me, if asked to name the main obstacle to the performance of my plays, would unhesitatingly and unanimously reply 'The author.' And I confess that though as a matter of business I wish my plays to be performed, as a matter of instinct I fight against the inevitable misrepresentation of them with all the subtlety needed to conceal my ill will from myself as well as from the manager.

The main difficulty, of course, is the incapacity for serious drama of thousands of playgoers of all classes whose shillings and half guineas will buy as much in the market as if they delighted in the highest art. But with them I must frankly take the superior position. I know that many managers are wholly dependent on them, and that no manager is wholly independent of them; but I can no more write what they want than Joachim[6] can put aside his fiddle and oblige a happy company of beanfeasters with a marching tune on the German concertina. They must keep away from my plays: that is all.

There is no reason, however, why I should take this haughty attitude towards those representative critics whose complaint is that my talent, though not unentertaining, lacks elevation of sentiment and seriousness of purpose. They can find, under the surface-brilliancy for which they give me credit, no coherent thought or sympathy, and accuse me, in various terms and degrees, of an inhuman and freakish wantonness; of preoccupation with 'the seamy side of life'; of paradox, cynicism, and eccentricity, reducible, as some contend, to a trite formula of treating bad as good and good as bad, important as trivial and trivial as important, serious as laughable and laughable as serious, and so forth. As to this formula I can only say that if any gentleman is simple enough to think that even a good comic opera can be produced by it, I invite him to try his hand, and see whether anything resembling one of my plays will reward him.

I could explain the matter easily enough if I chose; but the result would be that the people who misunderstand the plays would misunderstand the explanation ten times more. The particular exceptions taken are seldom more than symptoms of the underlying fundamental disagreement between the romantic morality of the critics and the natural morality of the plays. For example, I am quite aware that the much criticized Swiss officer in Arms and The Man is not a conventional stage soldier. He suffers from want of food and sleep; his nerves go to pieces after three days under fire, ending in the horrors of a rout and pursuit; he has found by experience that it is more important to have a few bits of chocolate to eat in the field than cartridges for his revolver. When many of my critics rejected these circumstances as fantastically improbable and cynically unnatural, it was not necessary to argue them into common sense: all I had to do was to brain them, so to speak, with the first half dozen military authorities at hand, beginning with the present Commander in Chief.[7] But when it proved that such unromantic (but all the more dramatic) facts implied to them a denial of the existence of courage, patriotism, faith, hope, and charity, I saw that it was not really mere matter of fact that was at issue between us. One strongly Liberal critic, the late Moy

6   Joseph Joachim (1831–1907), Hungarian violinist, composer, and conductor.
7   Lord Wolseley (see Introduction, pp. xxxviii–xxxix).

Thomas,[8] who had, in the teeth of a chorus of dissent, received my first play with the most generous encouragement, declared, when Arms and The Man was produced, that I had struck a wanton blow at the cause of liberty in the Balkan Peninsula by mentioning that it was not a matter of course for a Bulgarian in 1885 to wash his hands every day. He no doubt saw soon afterwards the squabble, reported all through Europe, between Stambouloff and an eminent lady of the Bulgarian court who took exception to his neglect of his fingernails. After that came the news of his ferocious assassination, with a description of the room prepared for the reception of visitors by his widow, who draped it with black, and decorated it with photographs of the mutilated body of her husband.[9] Here was a sufficiently sensational confirmation of the accuracy of my sketch of the theatrical nature of the first apings of western civilization by spirited races just emerging from slavery. But it had no bearing on the real issue between my critic and myself, which was, whether the political and religious idealism which had inspired Gladstone to call for the rescue of these Balkan principalities from the despotism of the Turk,[10] and converted miserably enslaved provinces into hopeful and gallant little States, will survive the general onslaught on idealism which is implicit, and indeed explicit, in Arms and The Man and the naturalist plays of the modern school. For my part I hope not; for idealism, which is only a flattering name for romance in politics and morals, is as obnoxious to me as romance in ethics or religion. In spite of a Liberal Revolution or two, I can no longer be satisfied with fictitious morals and fictitious good conduct, shedding fictitious glory on robbery, starvation, disease, crime, drink, war, cruelty, cupidity, and all the other commonplaces of civilization which drive men to the theatre to make foolish pretences that such things are progress, science, morals, religion, patriotism, imperial supremacy, national greatness and all the other names the newspapers call them. On the other hand, I see plenty of good in the world working itself out as fast as the idealists will allow it; and if they would only let it alone and learn to

---

8 W. Moy Thomas (1828–1910), theatre critic for the *Daily News*.

9 Bulgarian politician and sometime dictatorial premier Stefan Nikolov Stambolov (1854–95) was attacked on 15 July 1895 and died three days later.

10 Liberal politician William E. Gladstone (1809–98) created a public outcry when he published *Bulgarian Horrors and the Questions of the East* (1876) which publicized Turkish atrocities committed during the suppression of a Bulgarian uprising in 1876. Little was done immediately, although Bulgarian autonomy was recognized later by the Congress of Berlin (1878).

respect reality, which would include the beneficial exercise of respecting themselves, and incidentally respecting me, we should all get along much better and faster. At all events, I do not see moral chaos and anarchy as the alternative to romantic convention; and I am not going to pretend I do merely to please the people who are convinced that the world is held together only by the force of unanimous, strenuous, eloquent, trumpet-tongued lying. To me the tragedy and comedy of life lie in the consequences, sometimes terrible, sometimes ludicrous, of our persistent attempts to found our institutions on the ideals suggested to our imaginations by our half-satisfied passions, instead of on a genuinely scientific natural history. And with that hint as to what I am driving at, I withdraw and ring up the curtain.